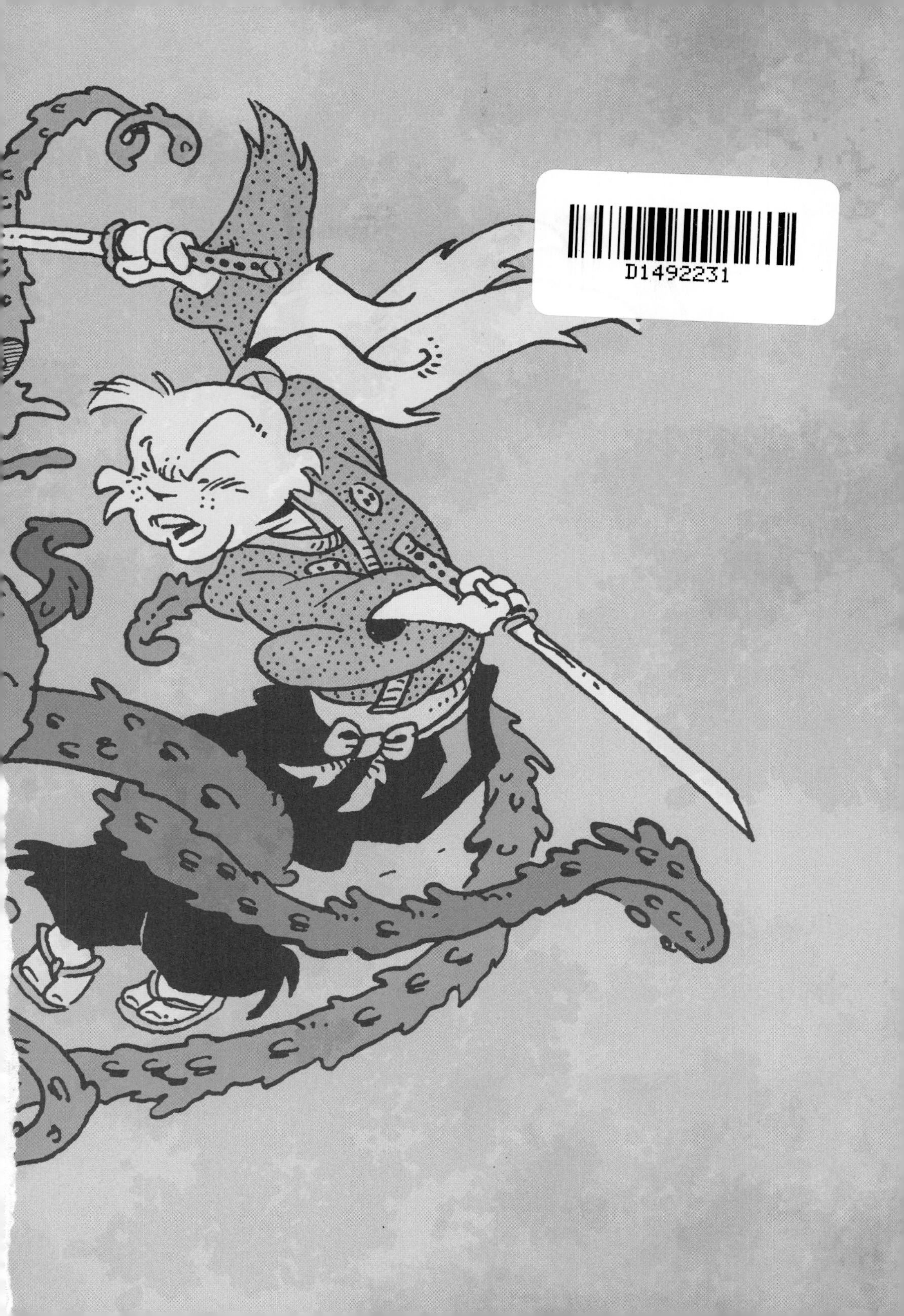

USAGI
YOKA
YOJIMBO ™

妖怪

Created, Written,
and Illustrated by

STAN SAKAI

DARK HORSE BOOKS®

FOR DR. SAM CONWAY,
YOU LITTLE COCKROACH.
KAMPAI.
乾杯

YOKAI

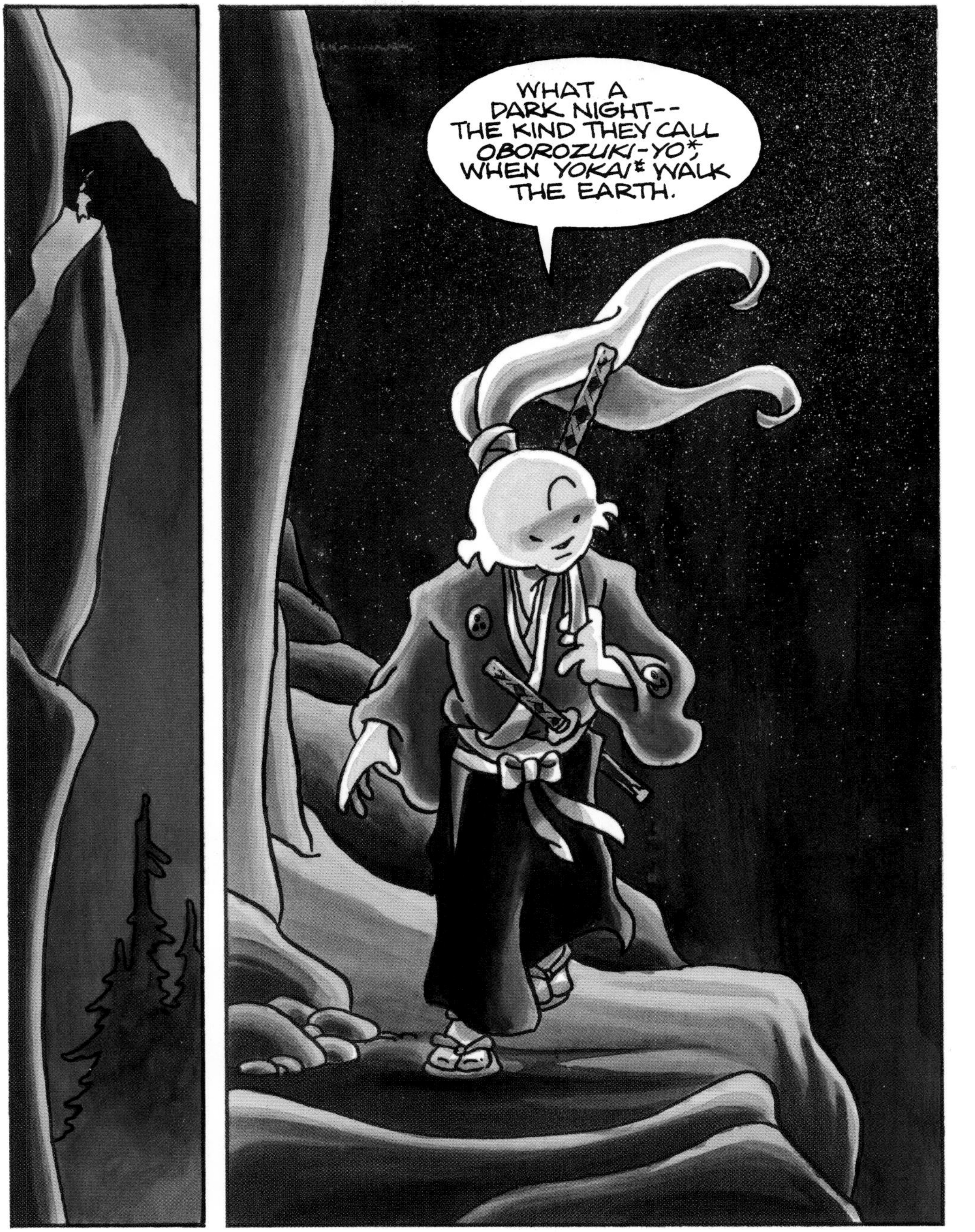
WHAT A DARK NIGHT-- THE KIND THEY CALL OBOROZUKI-YO*, WHEN YOKAI** WALK THE EARTH.

* NIGHT OF THE HAZY MOON
** HAUNTS

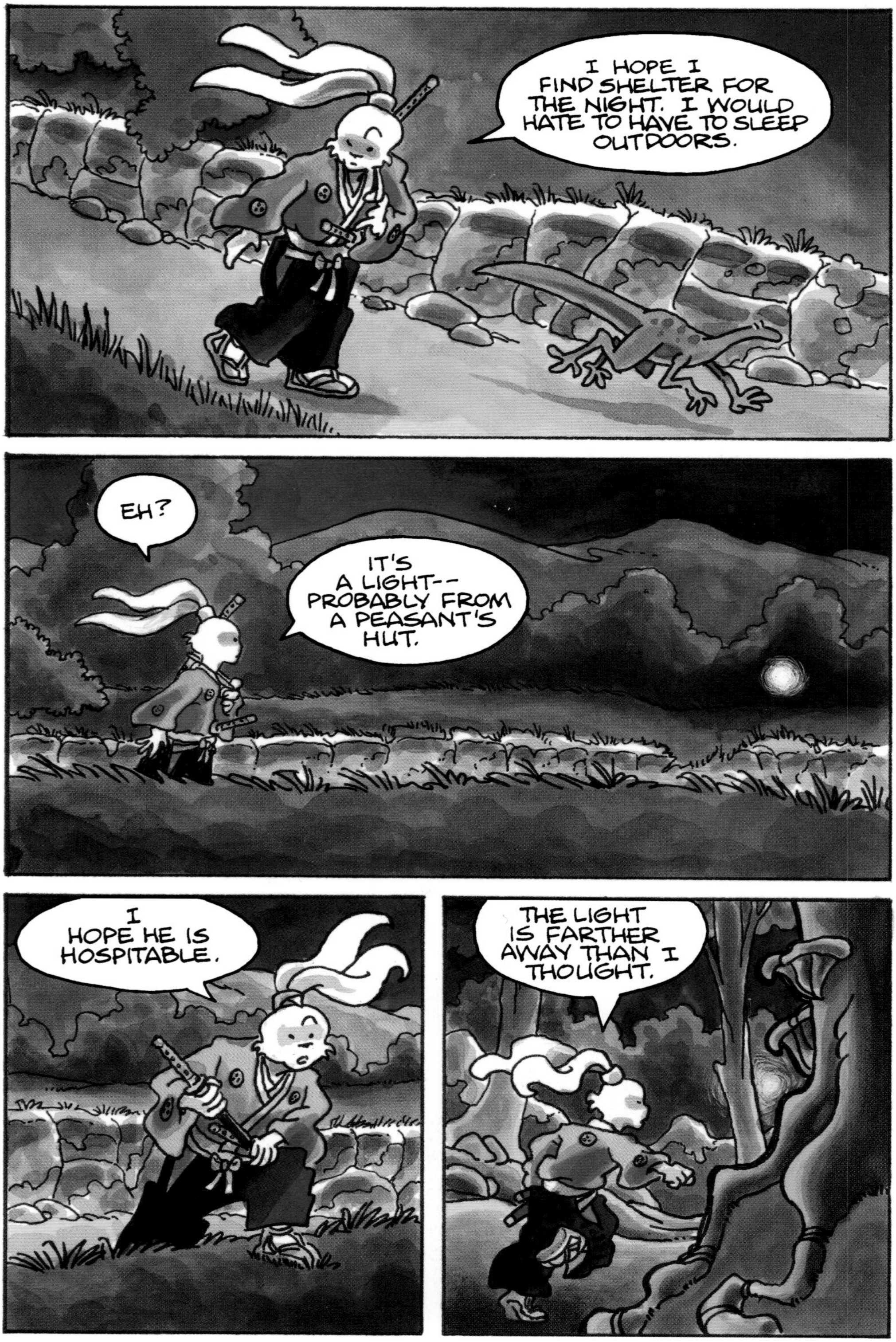
I HOPE I FIND SHELTER FOR THE NIGHT. I WOULD HATE TO HAVE TO SLEEP OUTDOORS.
EH?
IT'S A LIGHT-- PROBABLY FROM A PEASANT'S HUT.
I HOPE HE IS HOSPITABLE.
THE LIGHT IS FARTHER AWAY THAN I THOUGHT.

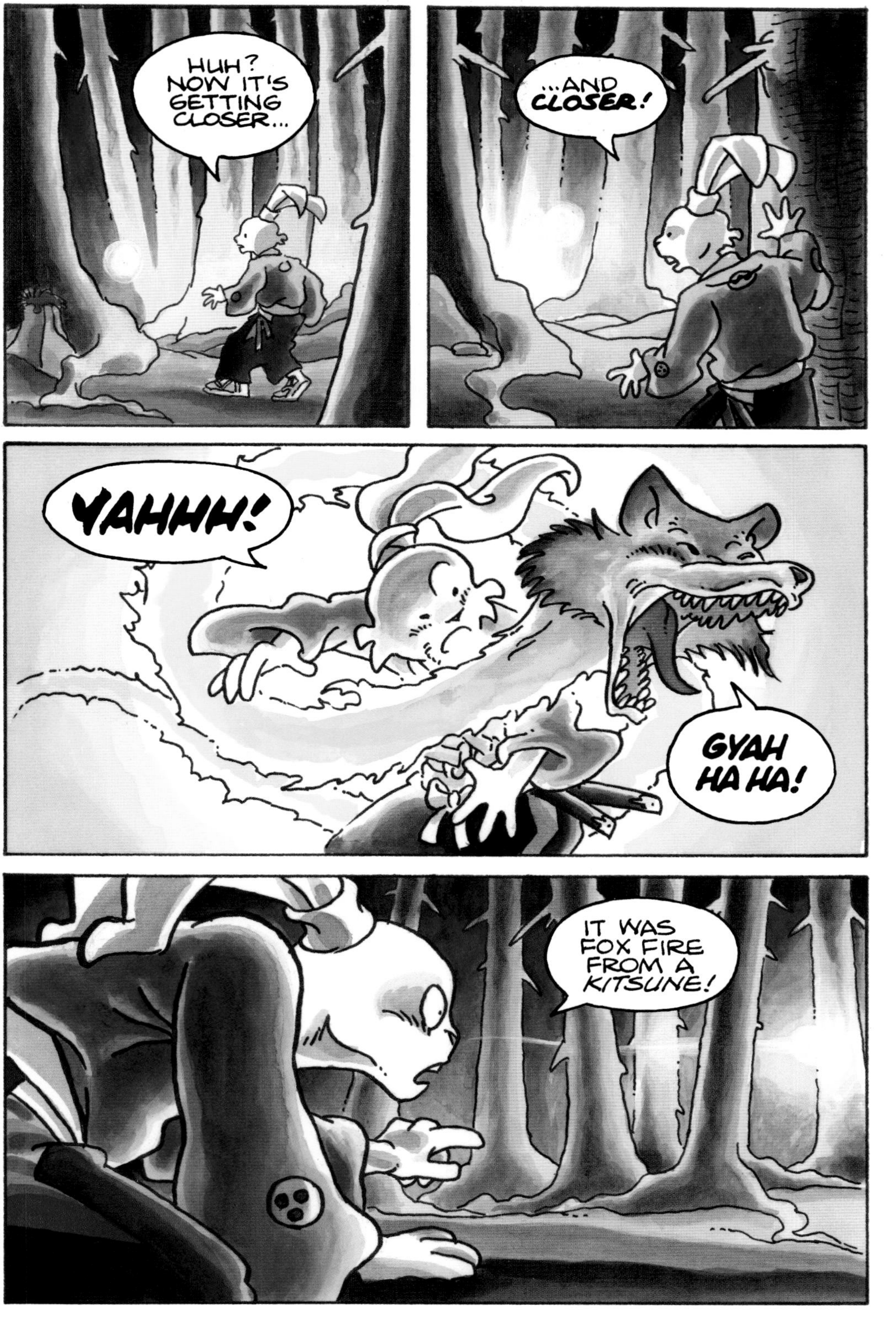
HUH? NOW IT'S GETTING CLOSER...
...AND CLOSER!
YAHHH!
GYAH HA HA!
IT WAS FOX FIRE FROM A KITSUNE!

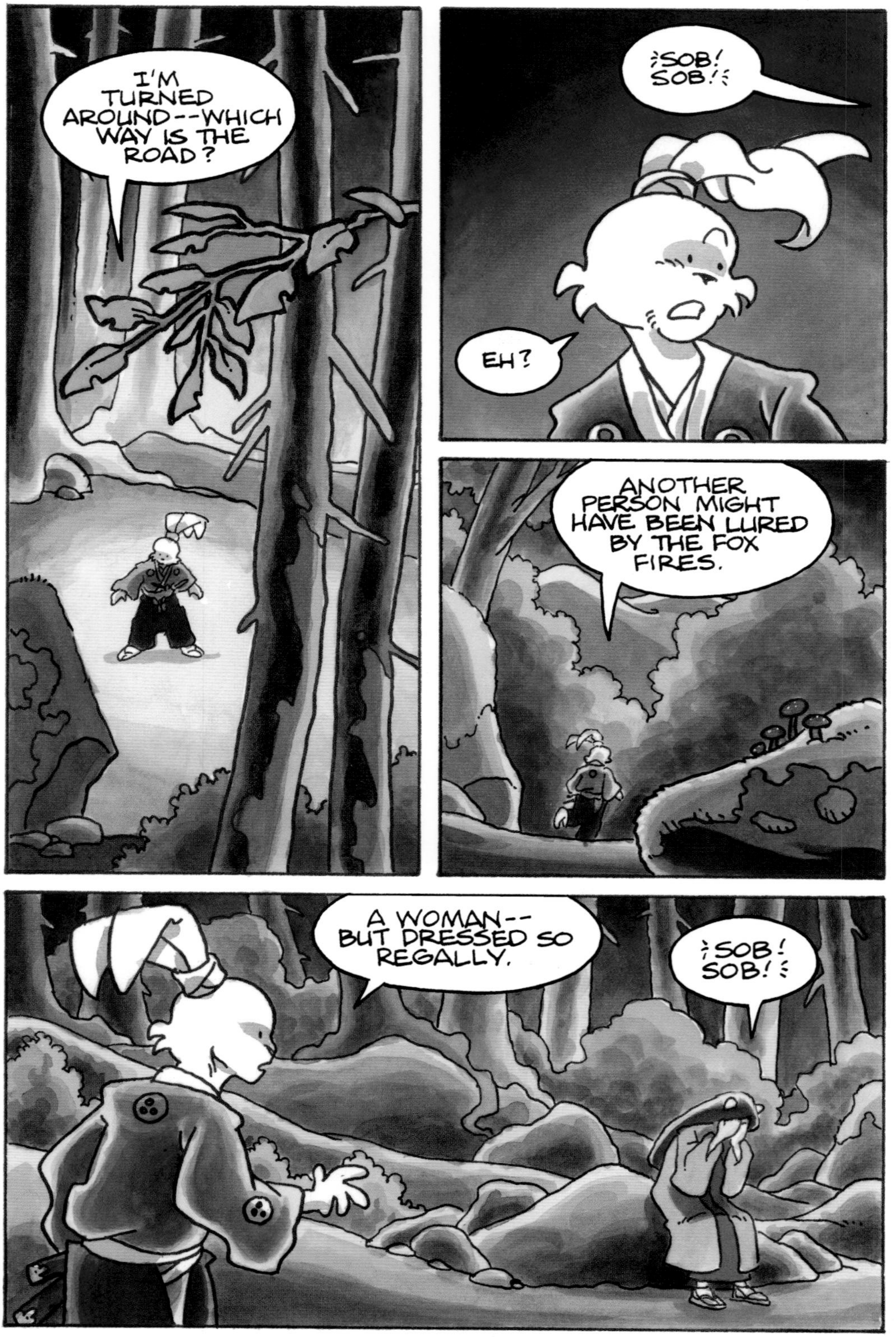

I'M TURNED AROUND--WHICH WAY IS THE ROAD?
SOB! SOB!
EH?
ANOTHER PERSON MIGHT HAVE BEEN LURED BY THE FOX FIRES.
A WOMAN--BUT DRESSED SO REGALLY.
SOB! SOB!

LADY...I AM MIYAMOTO USAGI. WERE YOU TRICKED BY A FOX AS I WAS?

YOU ARE KIND TO COME TO MY AID, USAGI-SAN. I AM FUJIMOTO HARUMI.

SHE'S BEAUTIFUL!

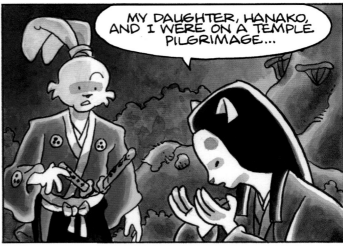

MY DAUGHTER, HANAKO, AND I WERE ON A TEMPLE PILGRIMAGE...

...WHEN A WILY FOX LURED US OUT HERE, THEN TOOK MY DAUGHTER DEEP INTO THE FOREST.

NOW I FEAR SHE IS GONE FOR GOOD. I CANNOT RETURN TO MY HUSBAND WITHOUT HER!

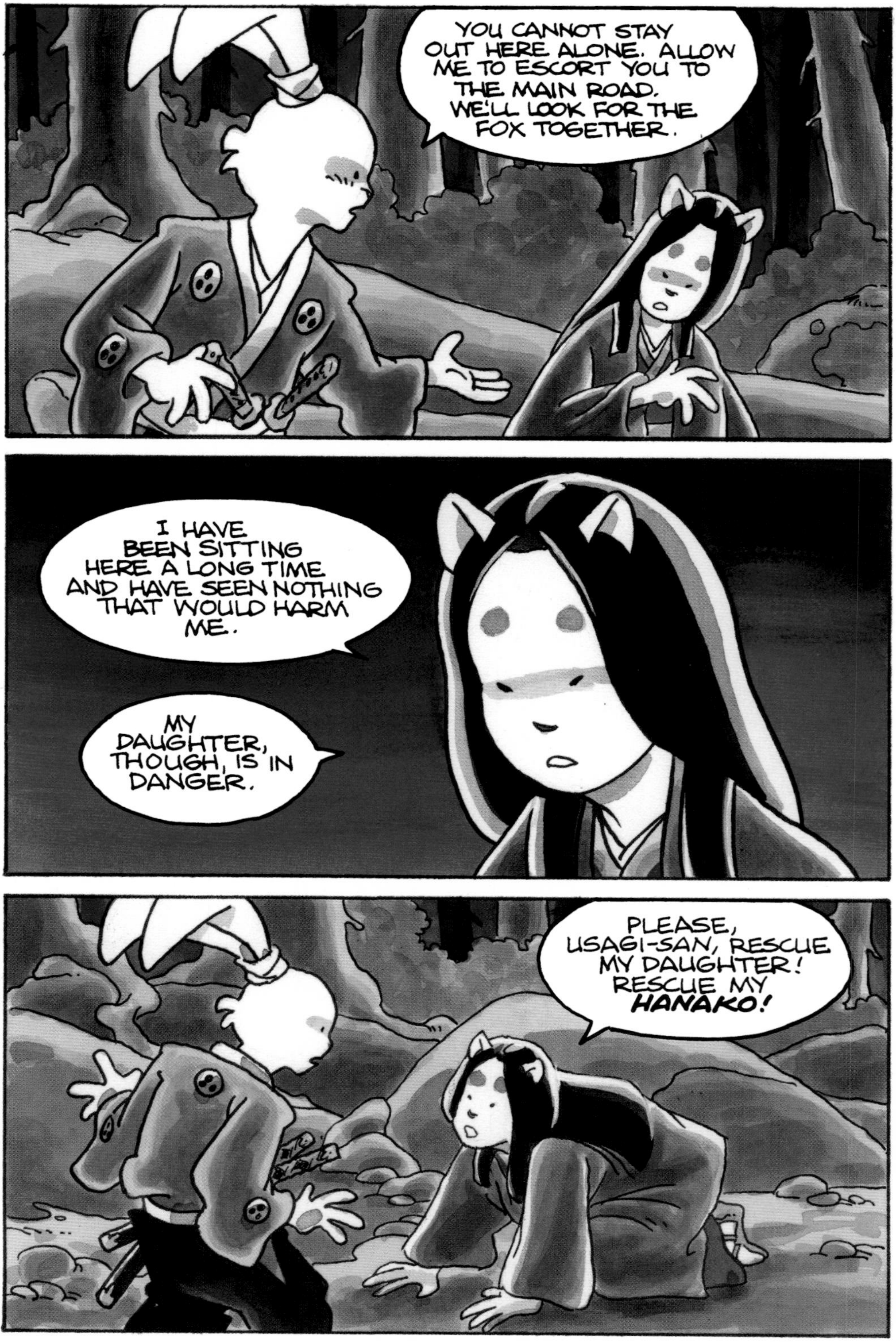
YOU CANNOT STAY OUT HERE ALONE. ALLOW ME TO ESCORT YOU TO THE MAIN ROAD. WE'LL LOOK FOR THE FOX TOGETHER.
I HAVE BEEN SITTING HERE A LONG TIME AND HAVE SEEN NOTHING THAT WOULD HARM ME.
MY DAUGHTER, THOUGH, IS IN DANGER.
PLEASE, USAGI-SAN, RESCUE MY DAUGHTER! RESCUE MY ***HANAKO!***

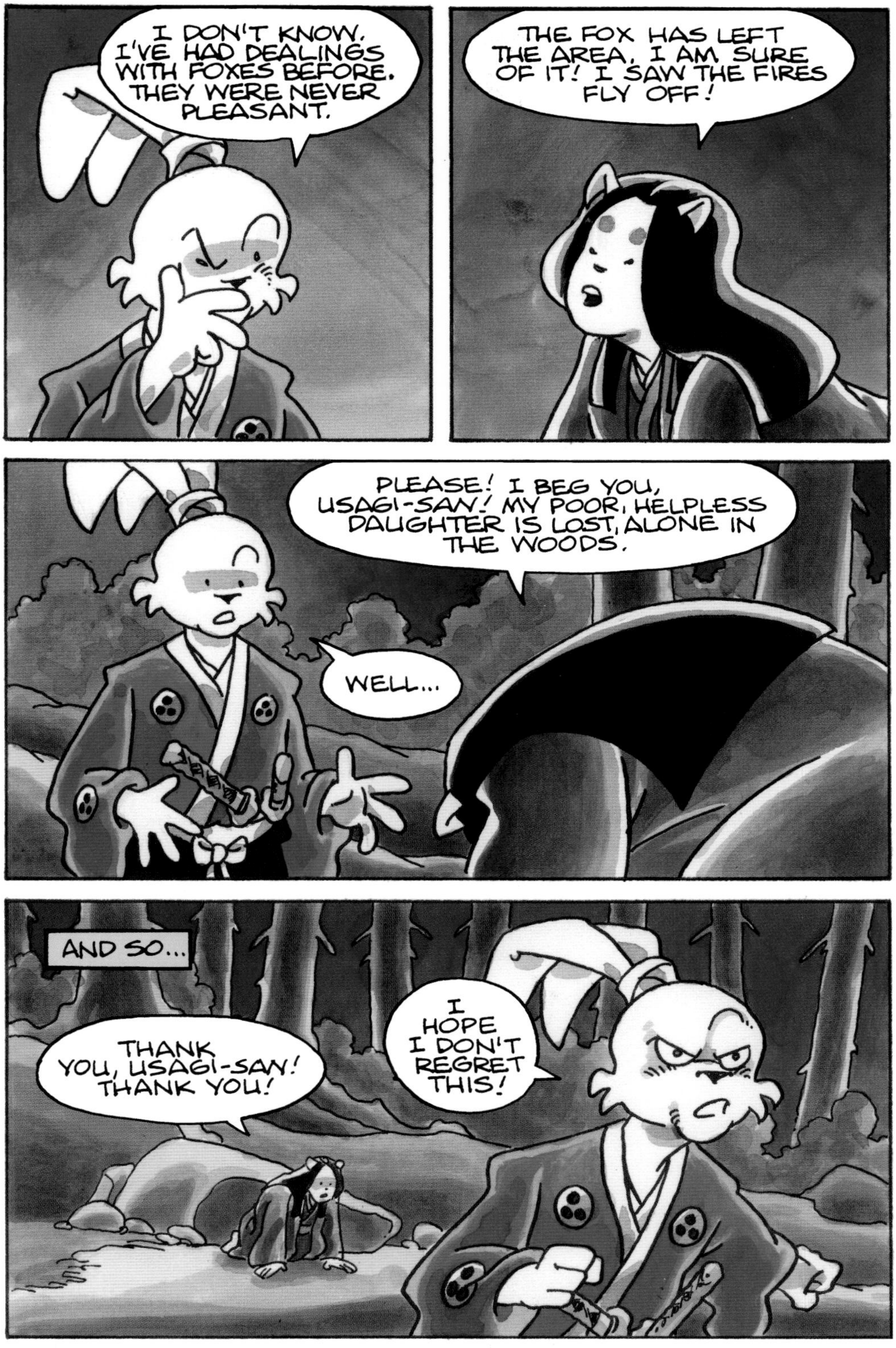
I DON'T KNOW. I'VE HAD DEALINGS WITH FOXES BEFORE. THEY WERE NEVER PLEASANT.
THE FOX HAS LEFT THE AREA, I AM SURE OF IT! I SAW THE FIRES FLY OFF!
PLEASE! I BEG YOU, USAGI-SAN! MY POOR, HELPLESS DAUGHTER IS LOST, ALONE IN THE WOODS.
WELL...
AND SO...
THANK YOU, USAGI-SAN! THANK YOU!
I HOPE I DON'T REGRET THIS!

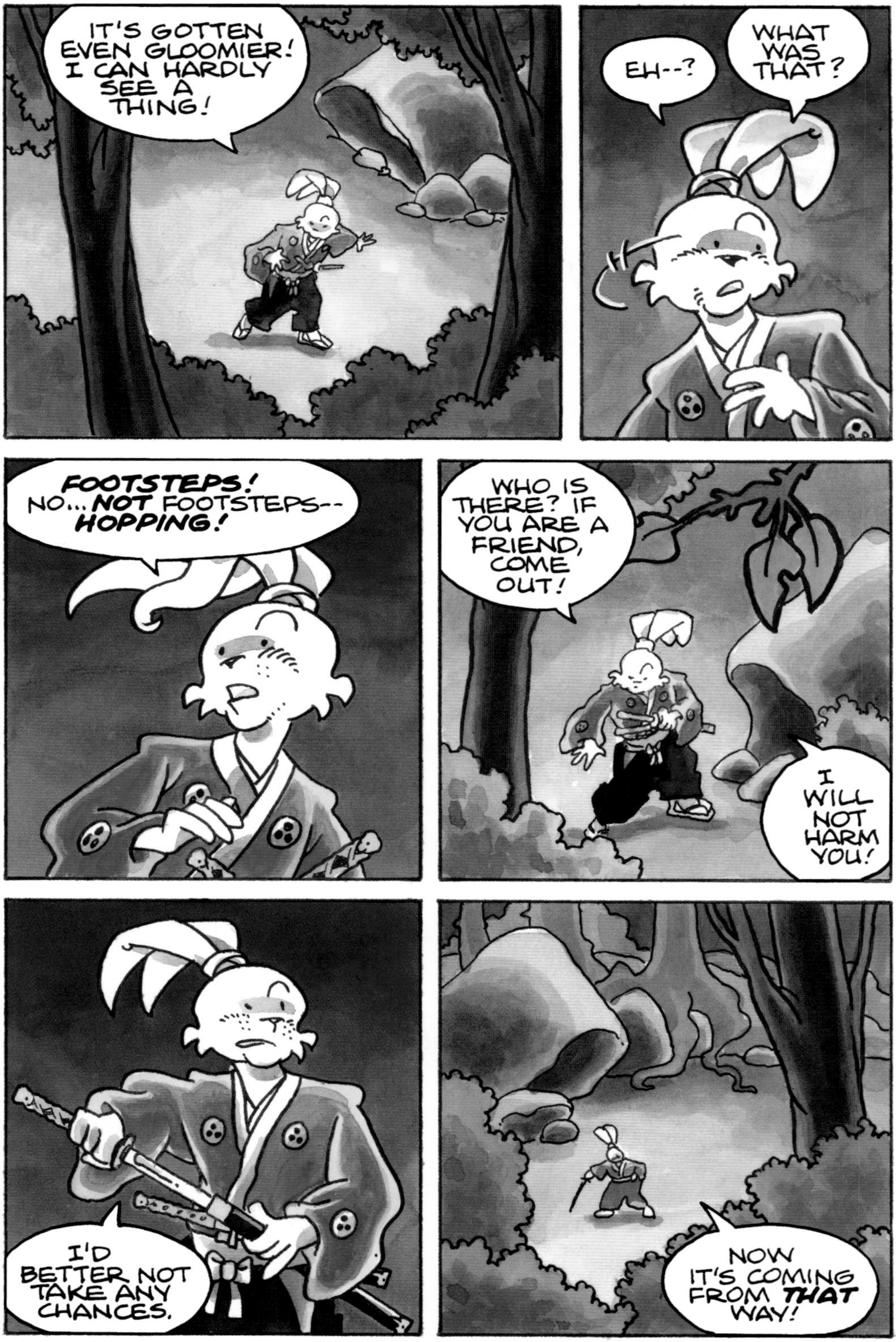

IT'S GOTTEN EVEN GLOOMIER! I CAN HARDLY SEE A THING!
EH--?
WHAT WAS THAT?
FOOTSTEPS! NO... **NOT** FOOTSTEPS-- **HOPPING!**
WHO IS THERE? IF YOU ARE A FRIEND, COME OUT!
I WILL NOT HARM YOU!
I'D BETTER NOT TAKE ANY CHANCES.
NOW IT'S COMING FROM **THAT** WAY!

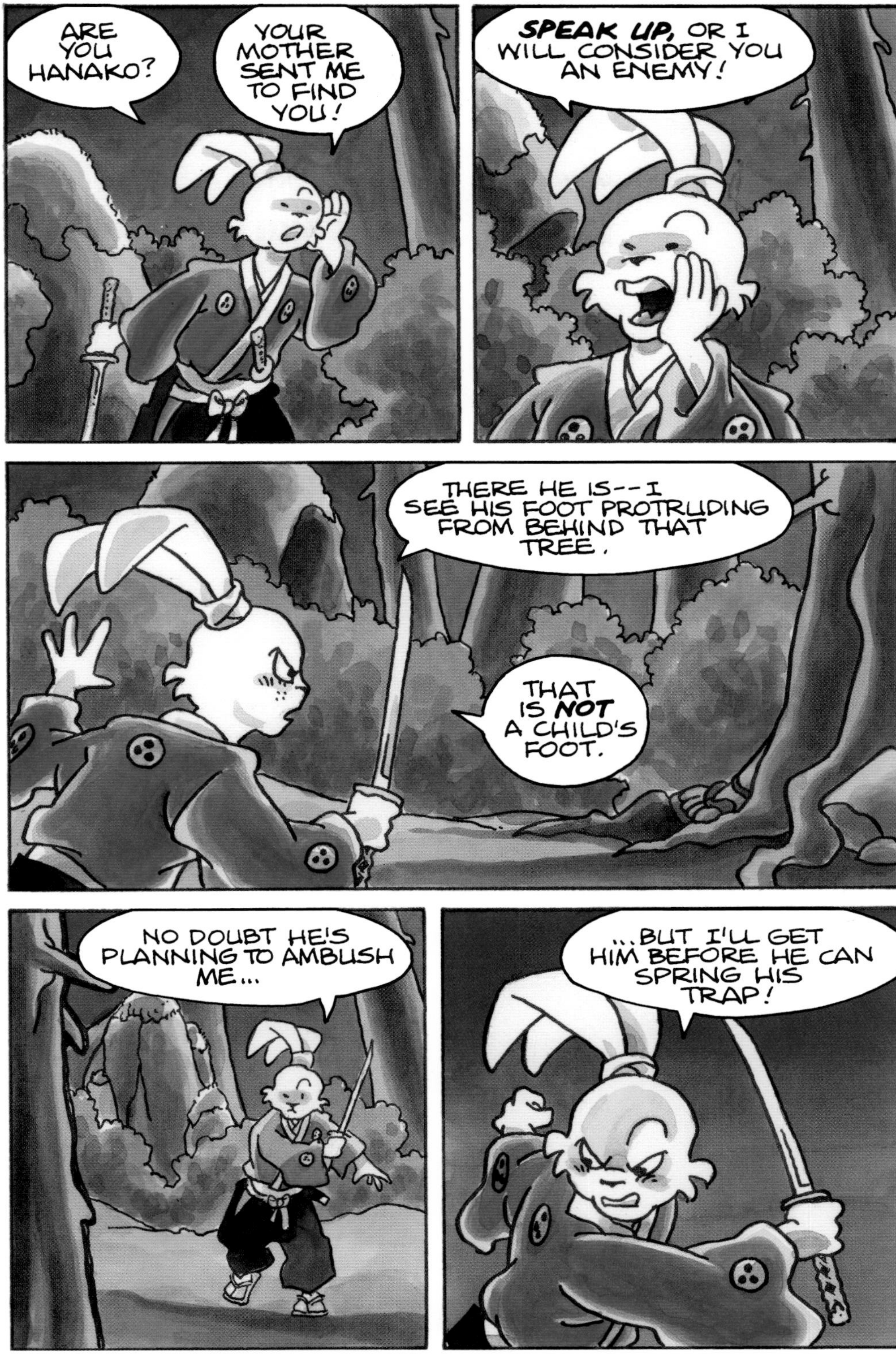
ARE YOU HANAKO?
YOUR MOTHER SENT ME TO FIND YOU!
SPEAK UP, OR I WILL CONSIDER YOU AN ENEMY!
THERE HE IS--I SEE HIS FOOT PROTRUDING FROM BEHIND THAT TREE.
THAT IS **NOT** A CHILD'S FOOT.
NO DOUBT HE'S PLANNING TO AMBUSH ME...
...BUT I'LL GET HIM BEFORE HE CAN SPRING HIS TRAP!

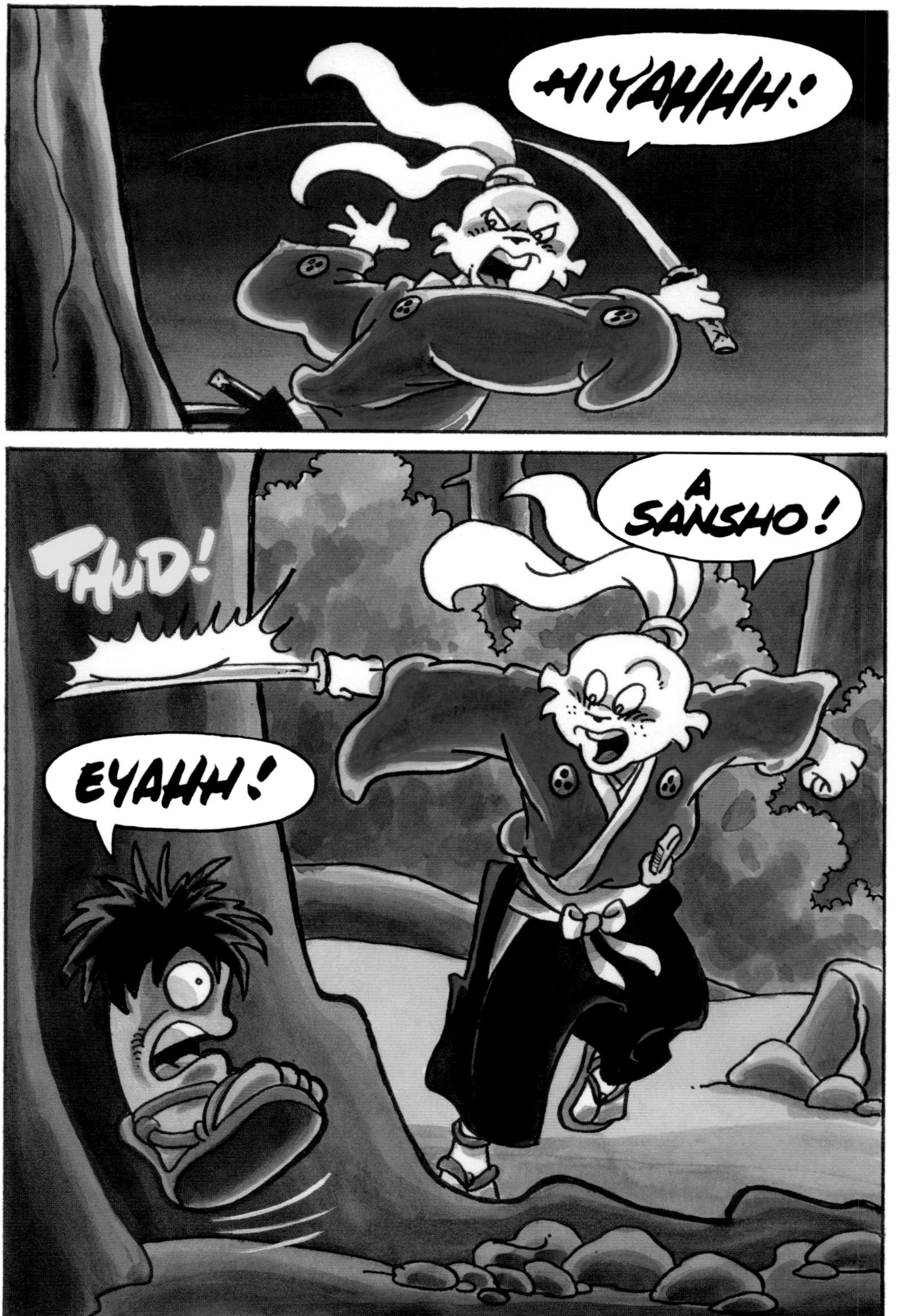
HIYAHHH!
A SANSHO!
THUD!
EYAHHH!

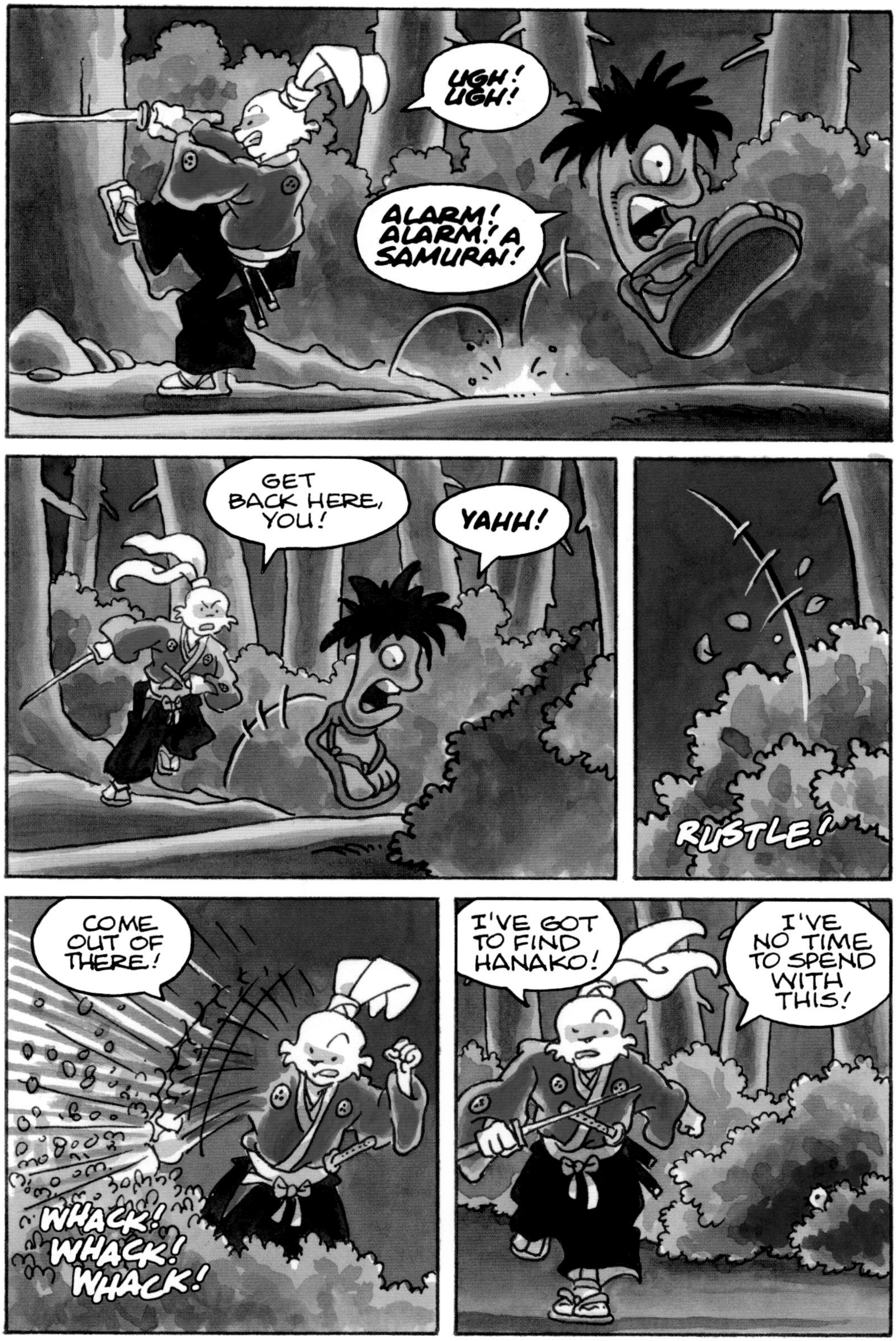
UGH! UGH!
ALARM! ALARM! A SAMURAI!
GET BACK HERE, YOU!
YAHH!
RUSTLE!
COME OUT OF THERE!
WHACK! WHACK! WHACK!
I'VE GOT TO FIND HANAKO!
I'VE NO TIME TO SPEND WITH THIS!

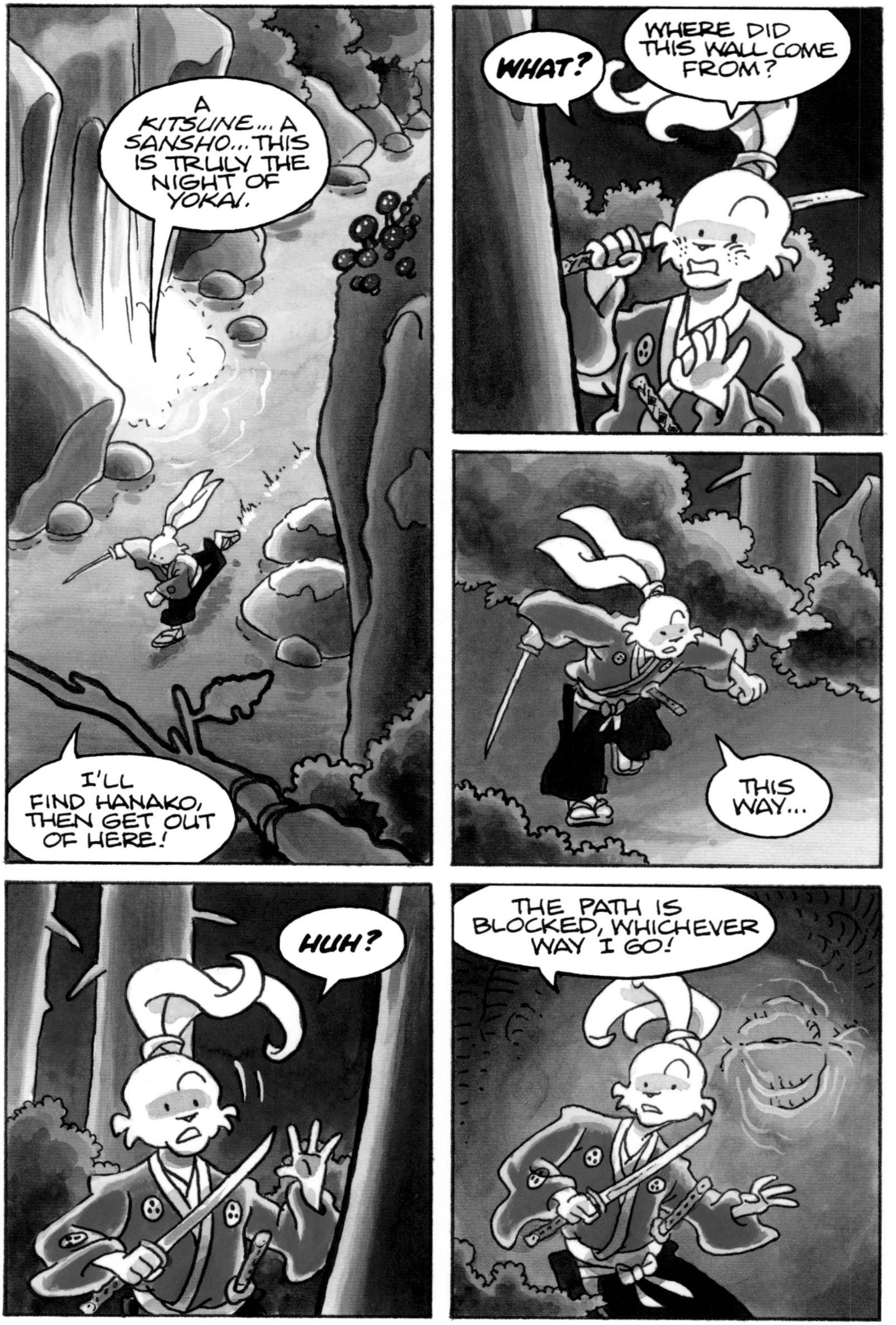
A KITSUNE... A SANSHO... THIS IS TRULY THE NIGHT OF YOKAI.
I'LL FIND HANAKO, THEN GET OUT OF HERE!
WHAT?
WHERE DID THIS WALL COME FROM?
THIS WAY...
HUH?
THE PATH IS BLOCKED, WHICHEVER WAY I GO!

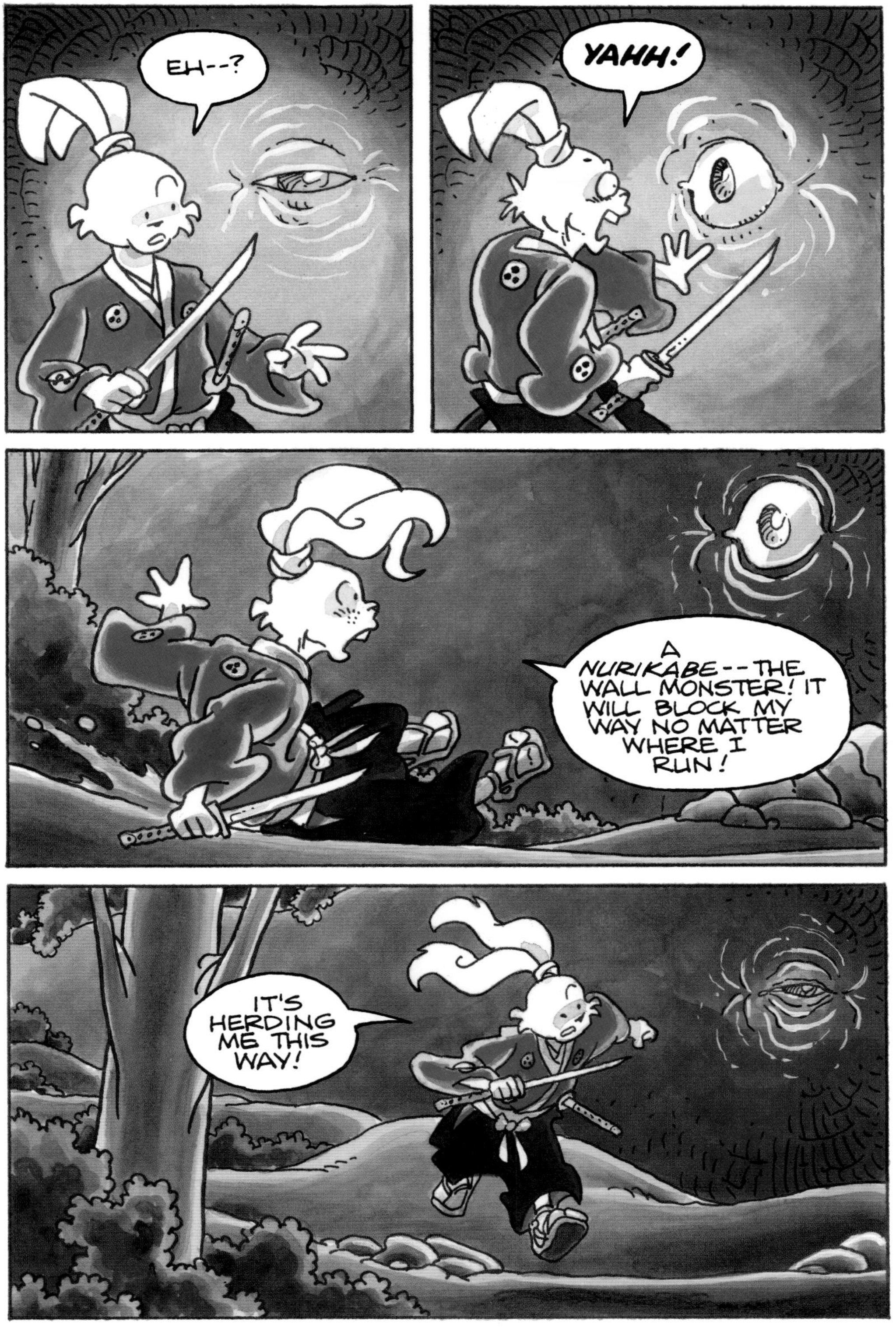
EH--?
YAHH!
A NURIKABE--THE WALL MONSTER! IT WILL BLOCK MY WAY NO MATTER WHERE I RUN!
IT'S HERDING ME THIS WAY!

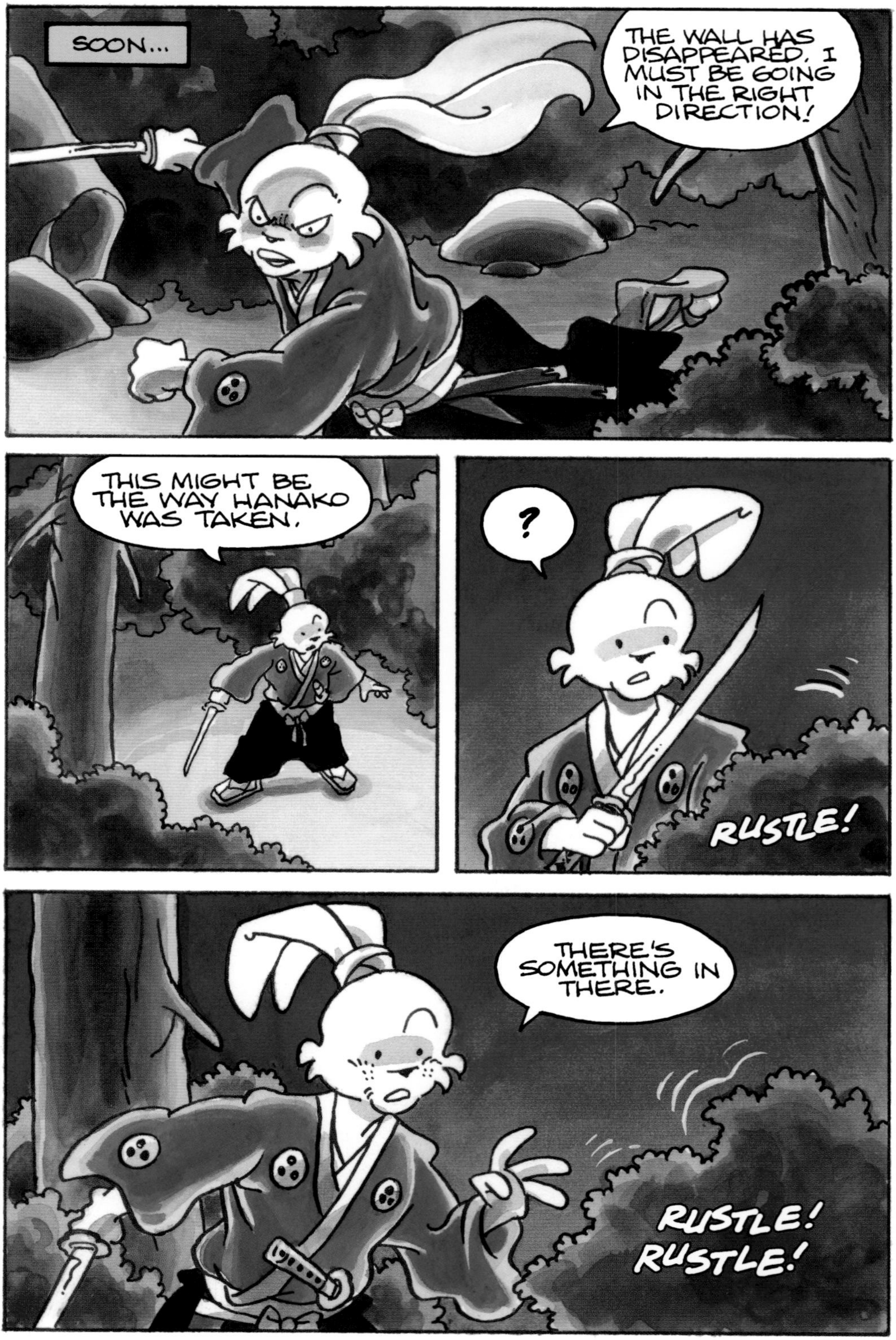
SOON...
THE WALL HAS DISAPPEARED. I MUST BE GOING IN THE RIGHT DIRECTION!
THIS MIGHT BE THE WAY HANAKO WAS TAKEN.
?
RUSTLE!
THERE'S SOMETHING IN THERE.
RUSTLE! RUSTLE!

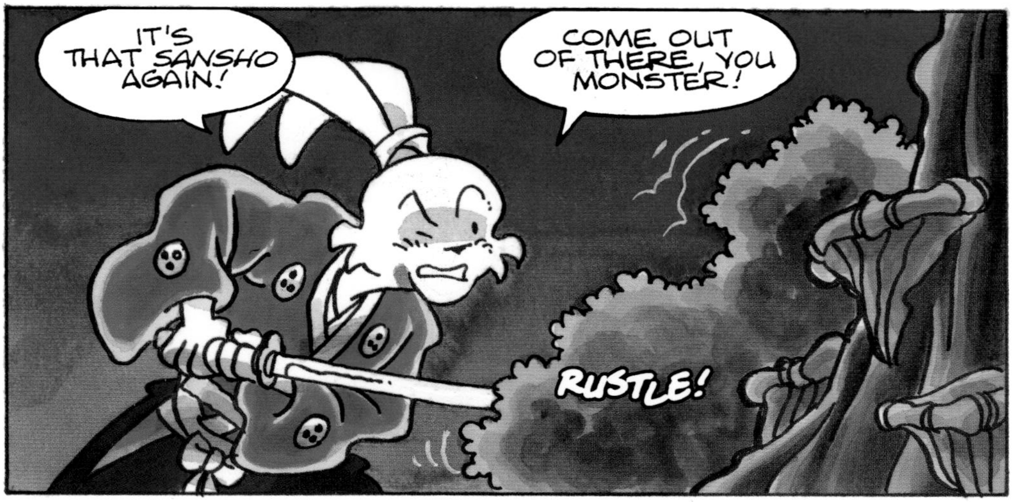
IT'S THAT SANSHO AGAIN!
COME OUT OF THERE, YOU MONSTER!
RUSTLE!

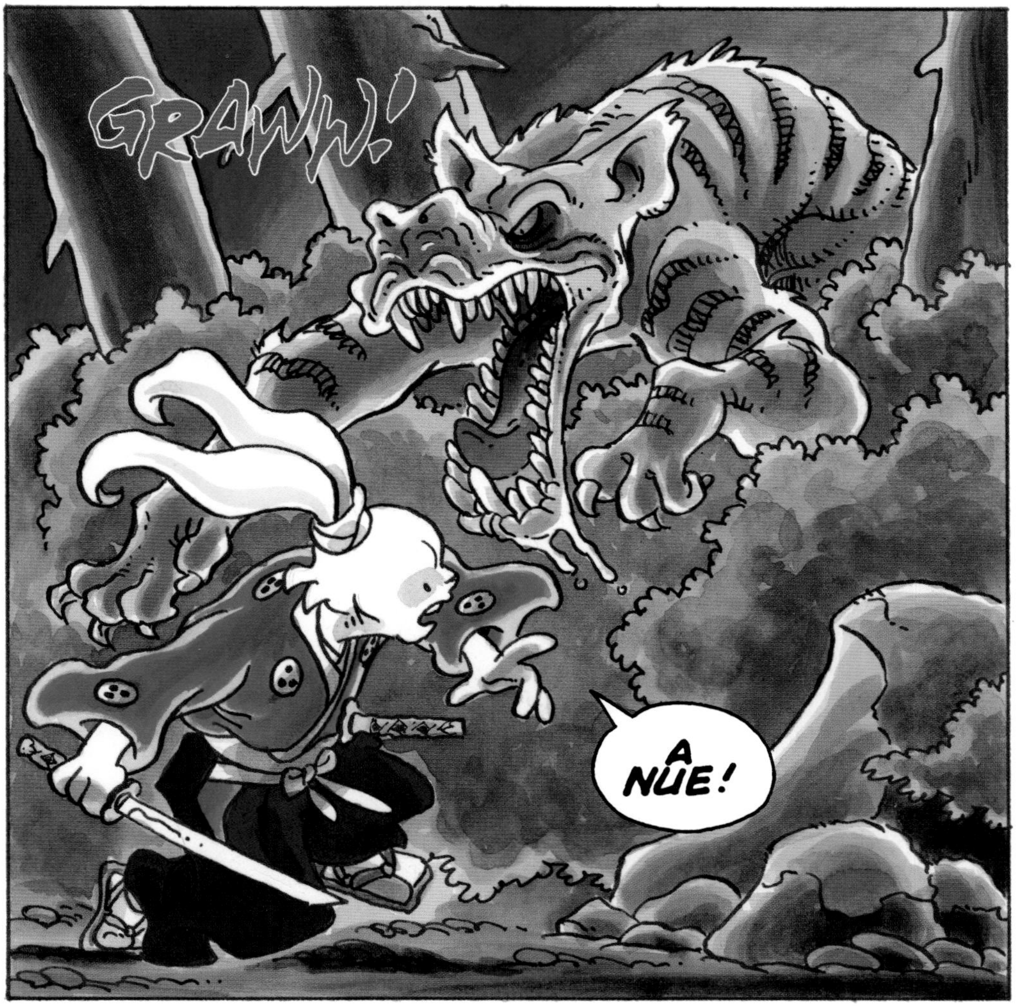
GRAWW!
A NUE!

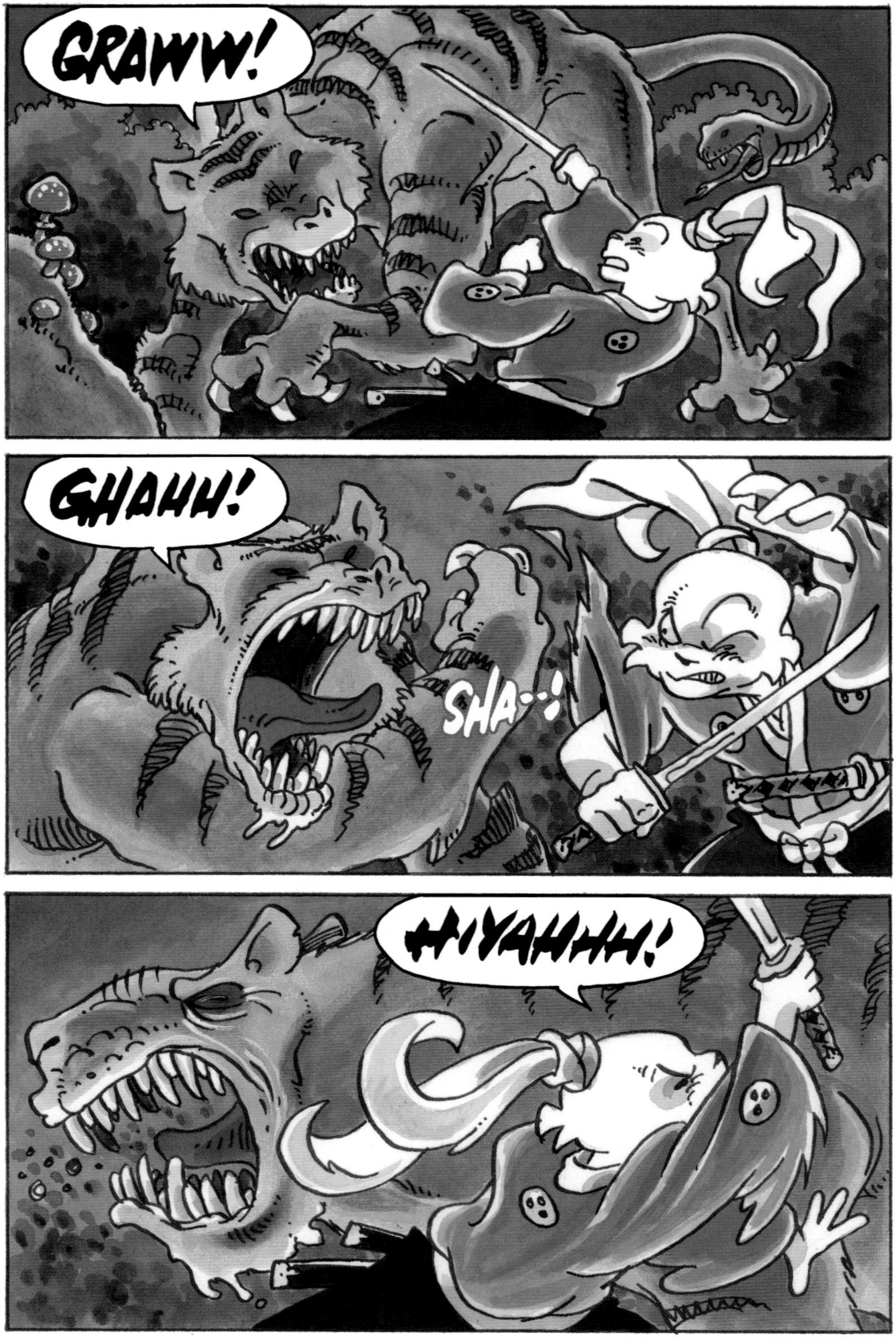
GRAWW!
GHAHH!
SHA--!
HIYAHHH!

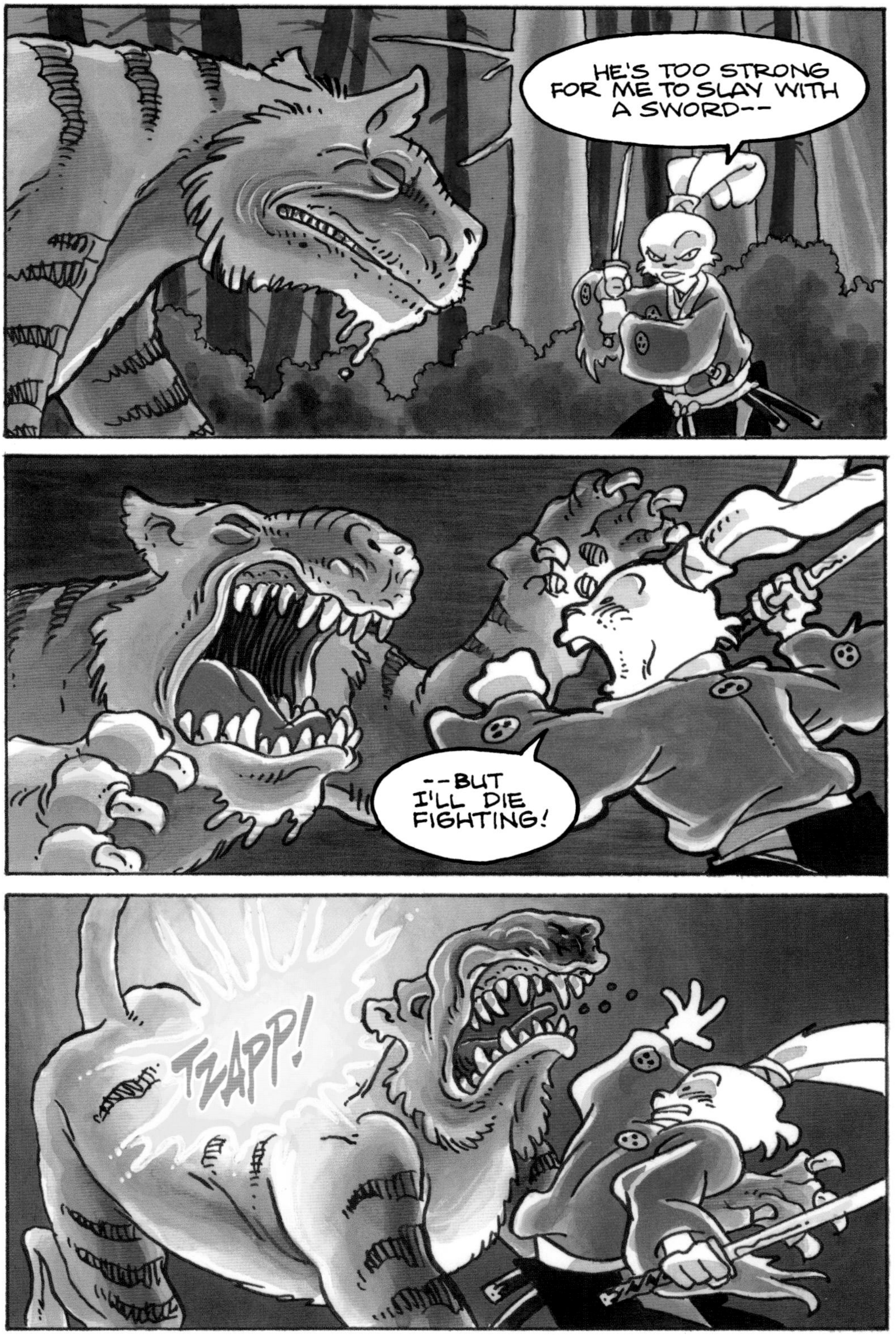
HE'S TOO STRONG FOR ME TO SLAY WITH A SWORD--
--BUT I'LL DIE FIGHTING!
TZAPP!

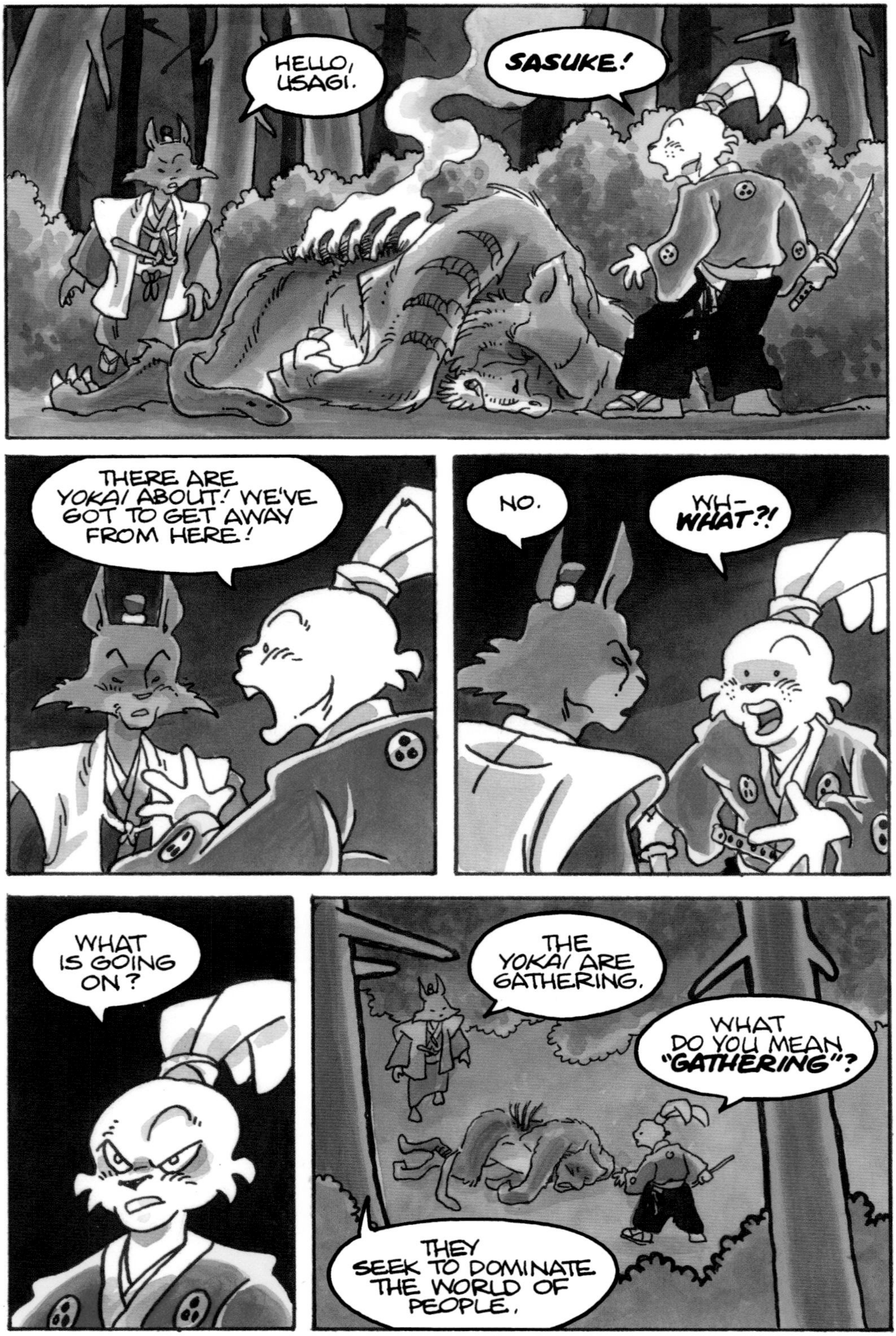

HELLO, USAGI.
SASUKE!
THERE ARE YOKAI ABOUT! WE'VE GOT TO GET AWAY FROM HERE!
NO.
WH- WHAT?!
WHAT IS GOING ON?
THE YOKAI ARE GATHERING.
WHAT DO YOU MEAN "GATHERING"?
THEY SEEK TO DOMINATE THE WORLD OF PEOPLE.

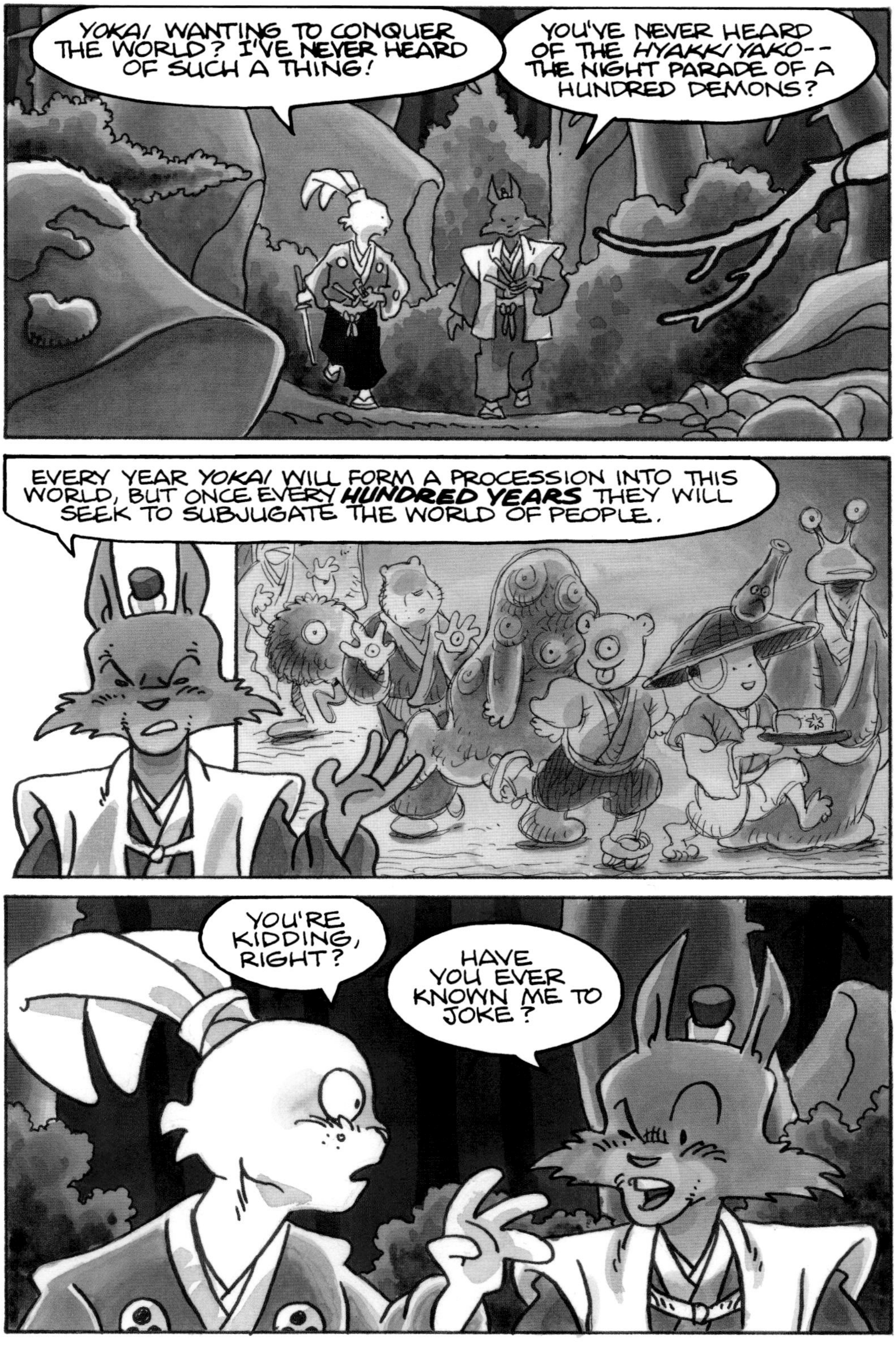
YOKAI WANTING TO CONQUER THE WORLD? I'VE NEVER HEARD OF SUCH A THING!
YOU'VE NEVER HEARD OF THE HYAKKI YAKO-- THE NIGHT PARADE OF A HUNDRED DEMONS?
EVERY YEAR YOKAI WILL FORM A PROCESSION INTO THIS WORLD, BUT ONCE EVERY HUNDRED YEARS THEY WILL SEEK TO SUBJUGATE THE WORLD OF PEOPLE.
YOU'RE KIDDING, RIGHT?
HAVE YOU EVER KNOWN ME TO JOKE?

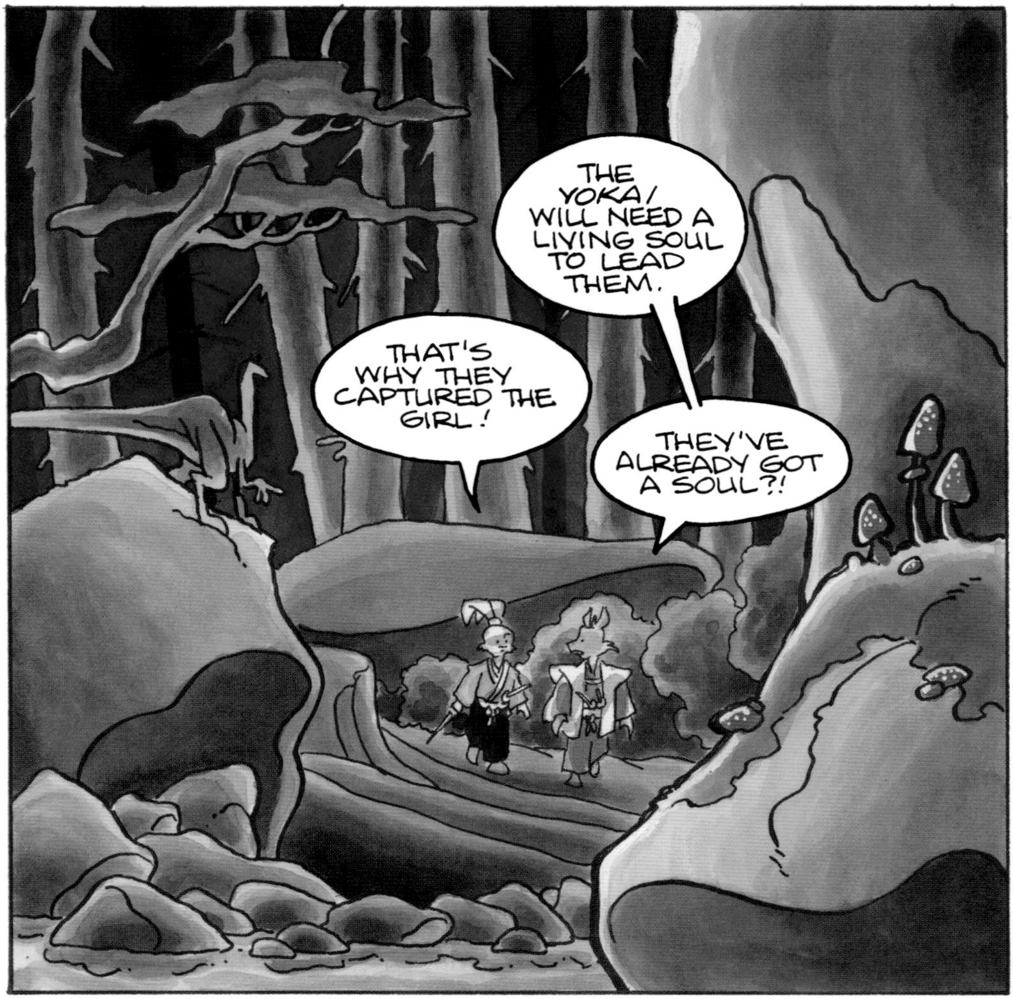
THE YOKAI WILL NEED A LIVING SOUL TO LEAD THEM.
THAT'S WHY THEY CAPTURED THE GIRL!
THEY'VE ALREADY GOT A SOUL?!

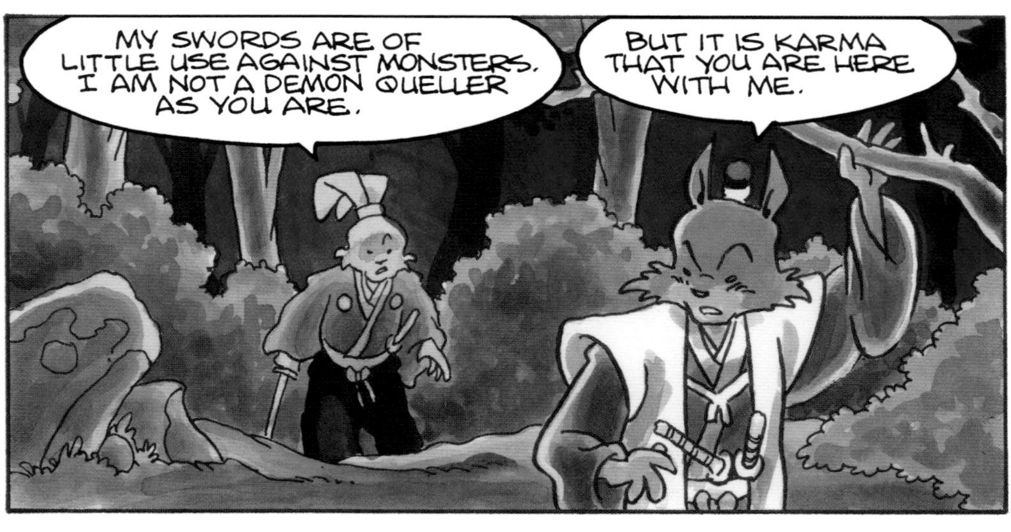
MY SWORDS ARE OF LITTLE USE AGAINST MONSTERS. I AM NOT A DEMON QUELLER AS YOU ARE.
BUT IT IS KARMA THAT YOU ARE HERE WITH ME.

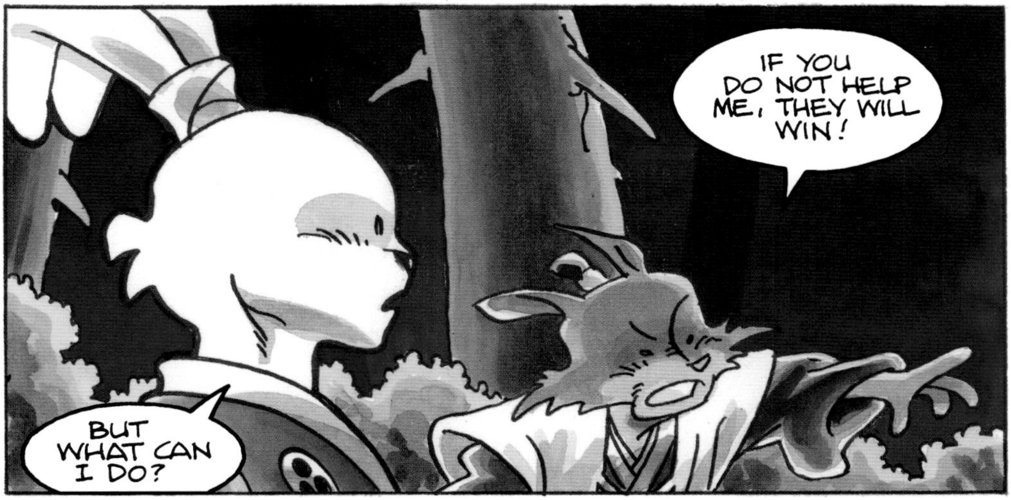
IF YOU DO NOT HELP ME, THEY WILL WIN!
BUT WHAT CAN I DO?

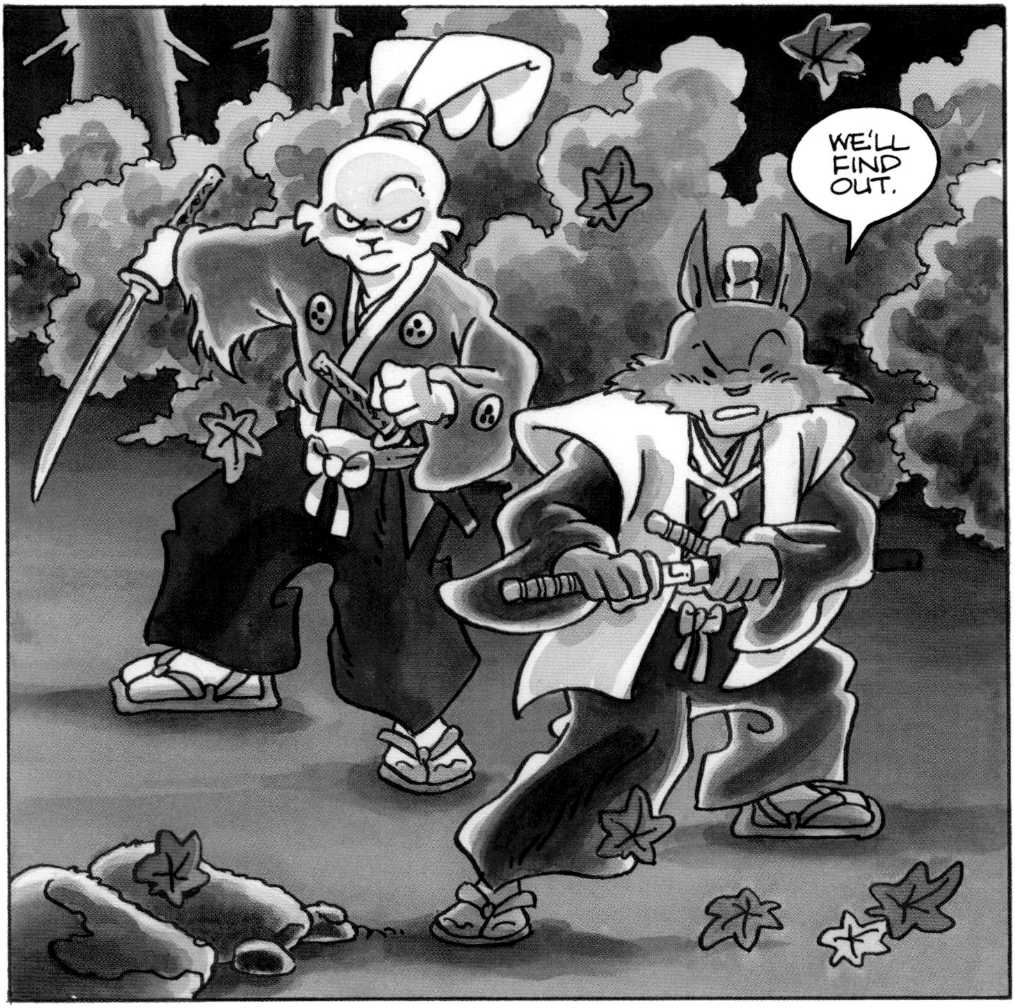
WE'LL FIND OUT.

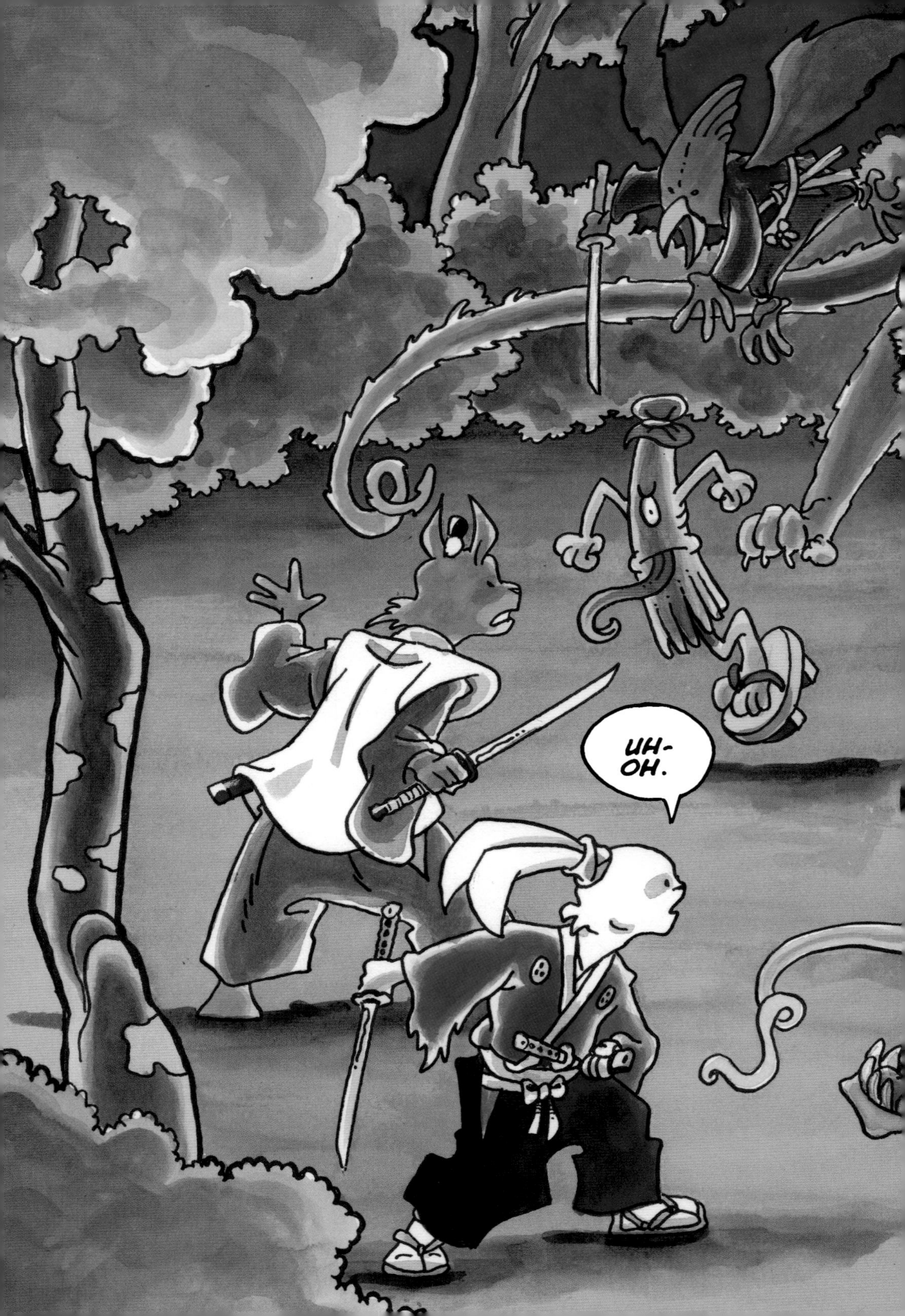
UH-OH.

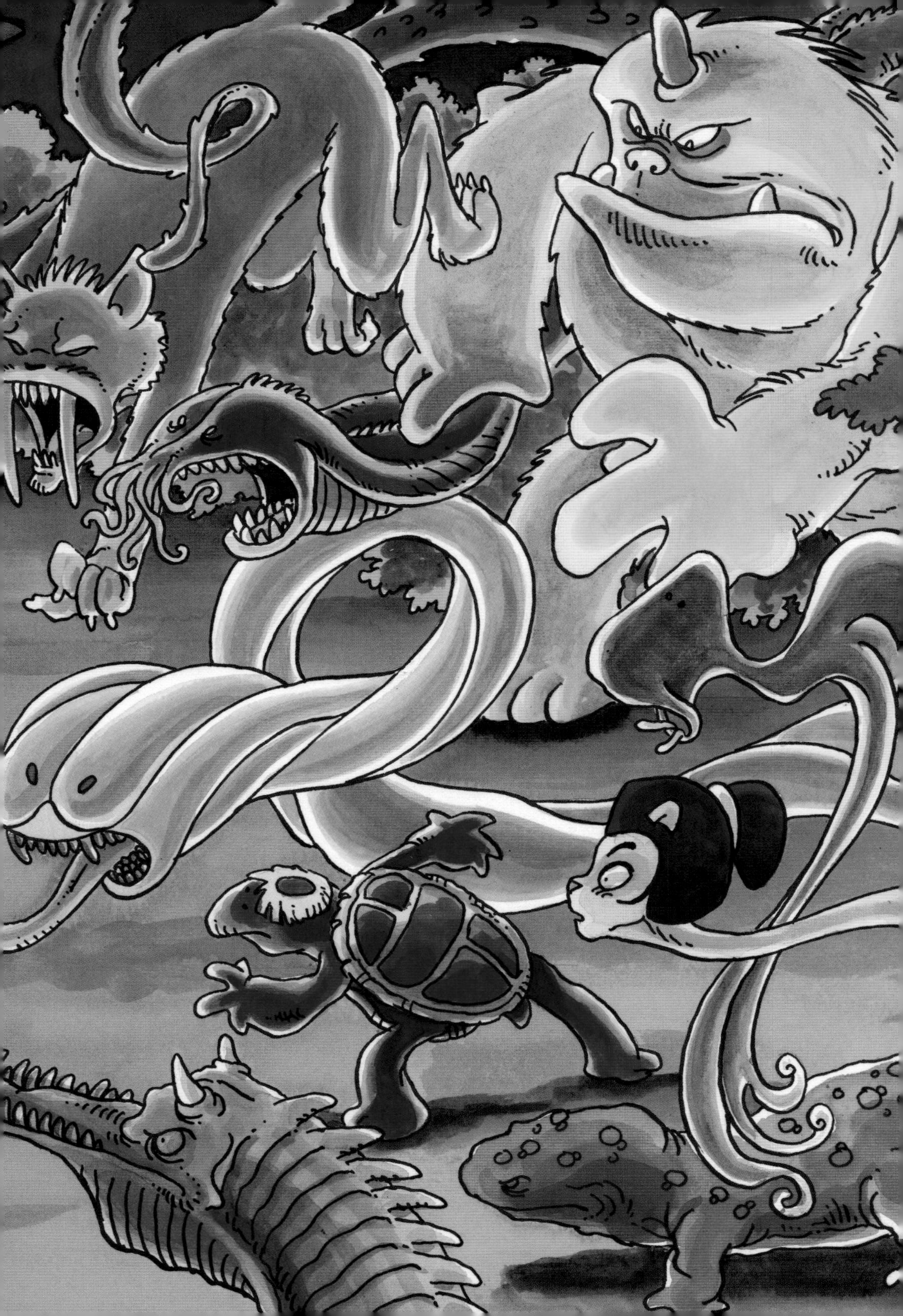

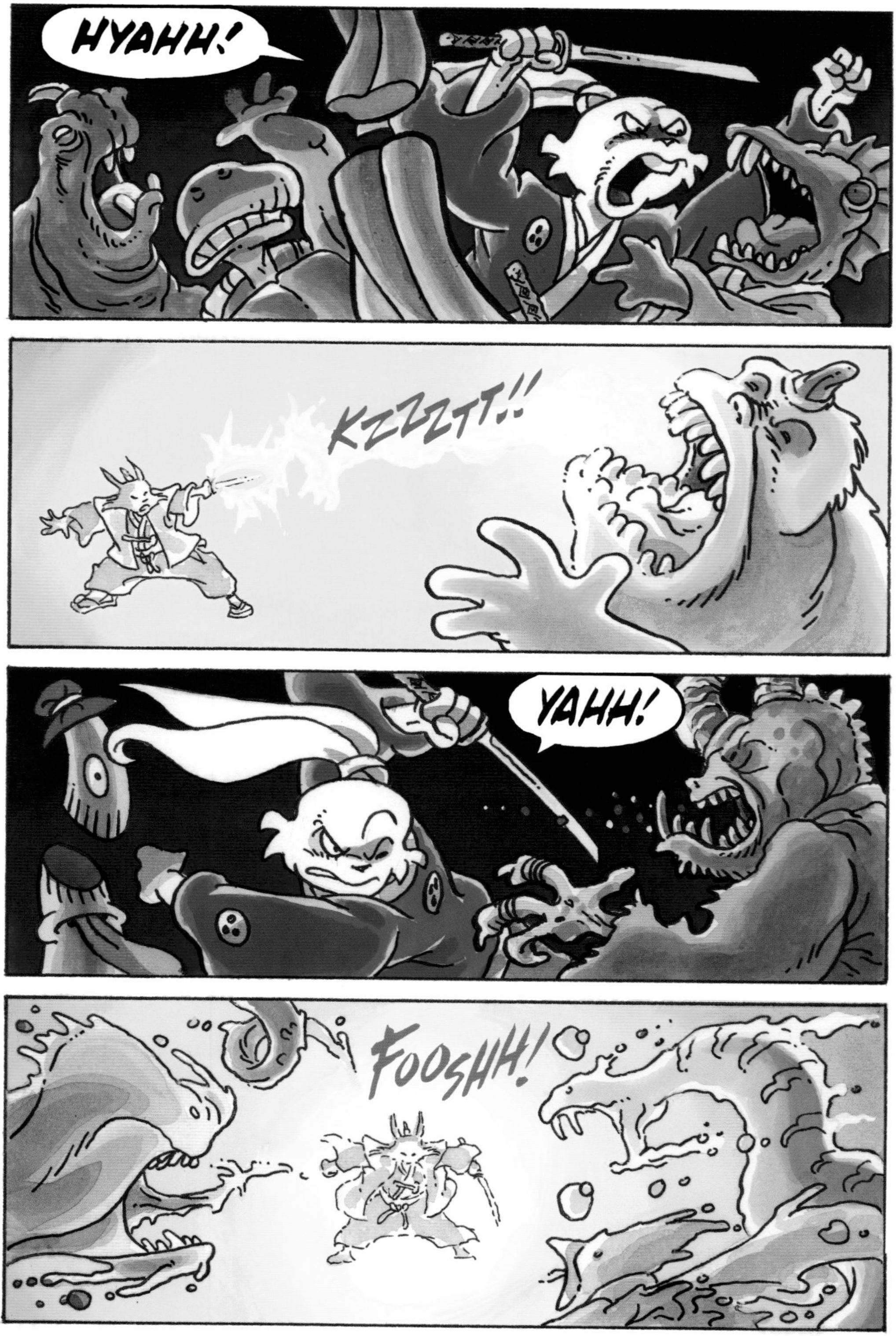
HYAHH!
KZZZTT!!
YAHH!
FOOSHH!

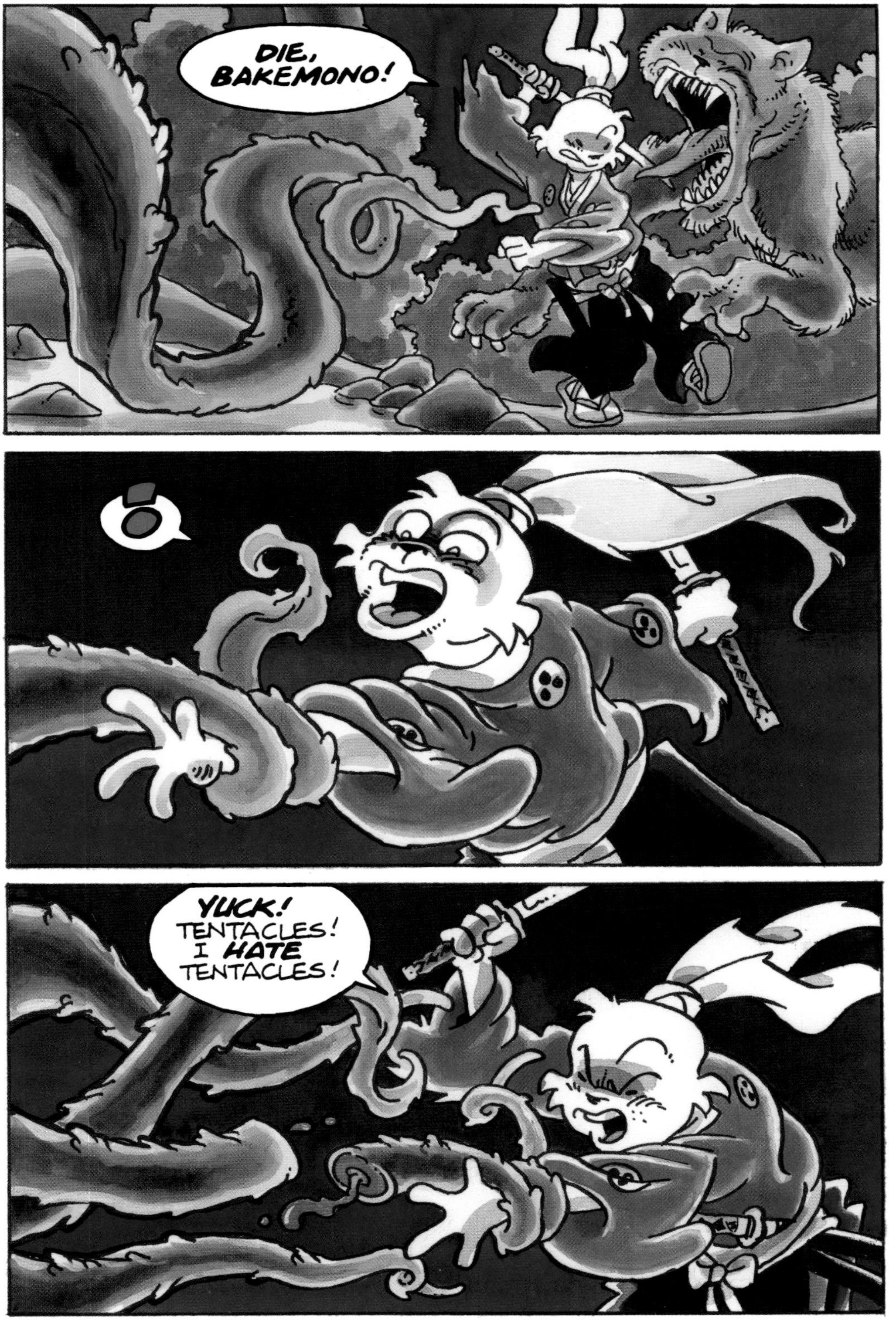
DIE, BAKEMONO!
YUCK! TENTACLES! I HATE TENTACLES!

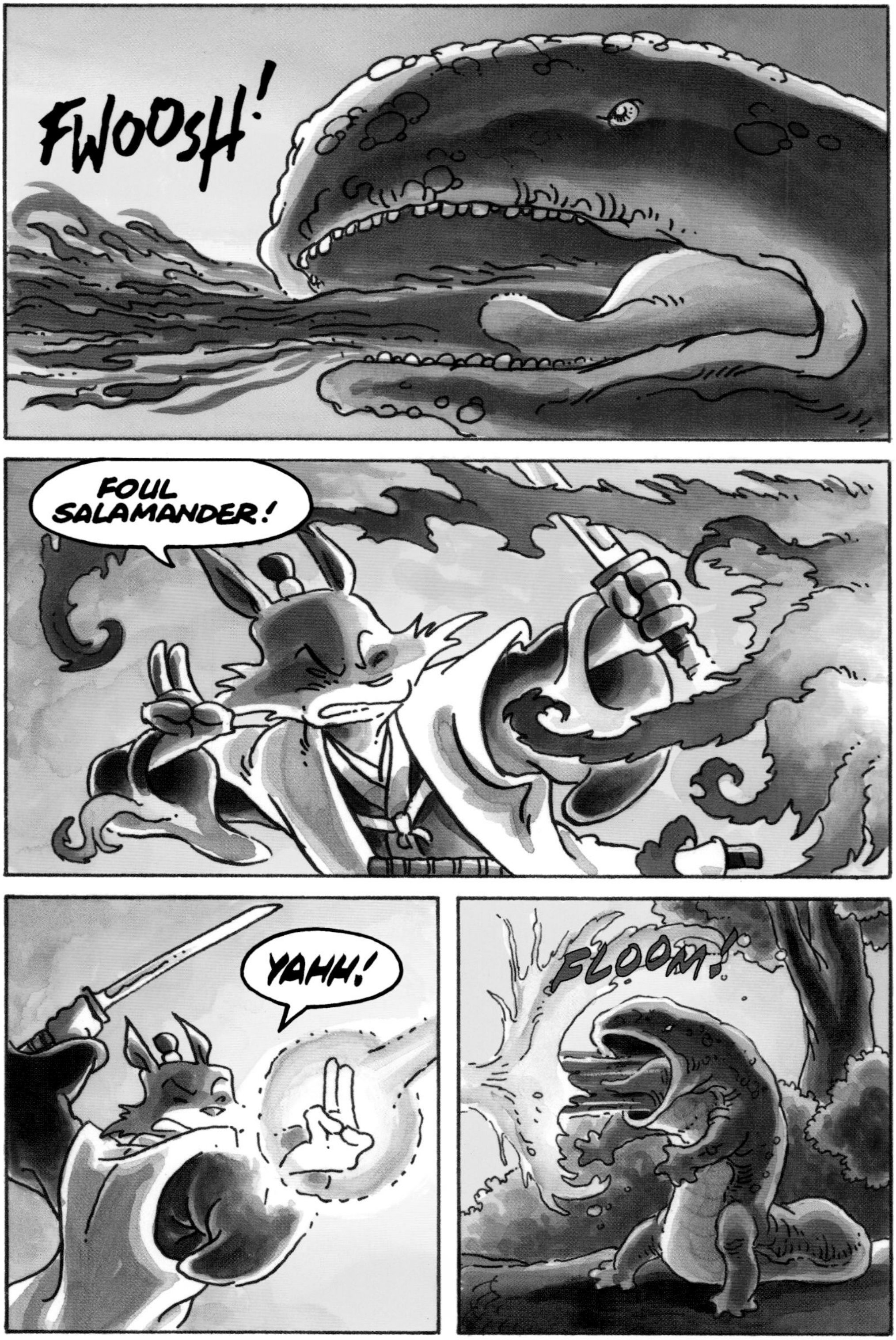
FWOOSH!
FOUL SALAMANDER!
YAHH!
FLOOM!

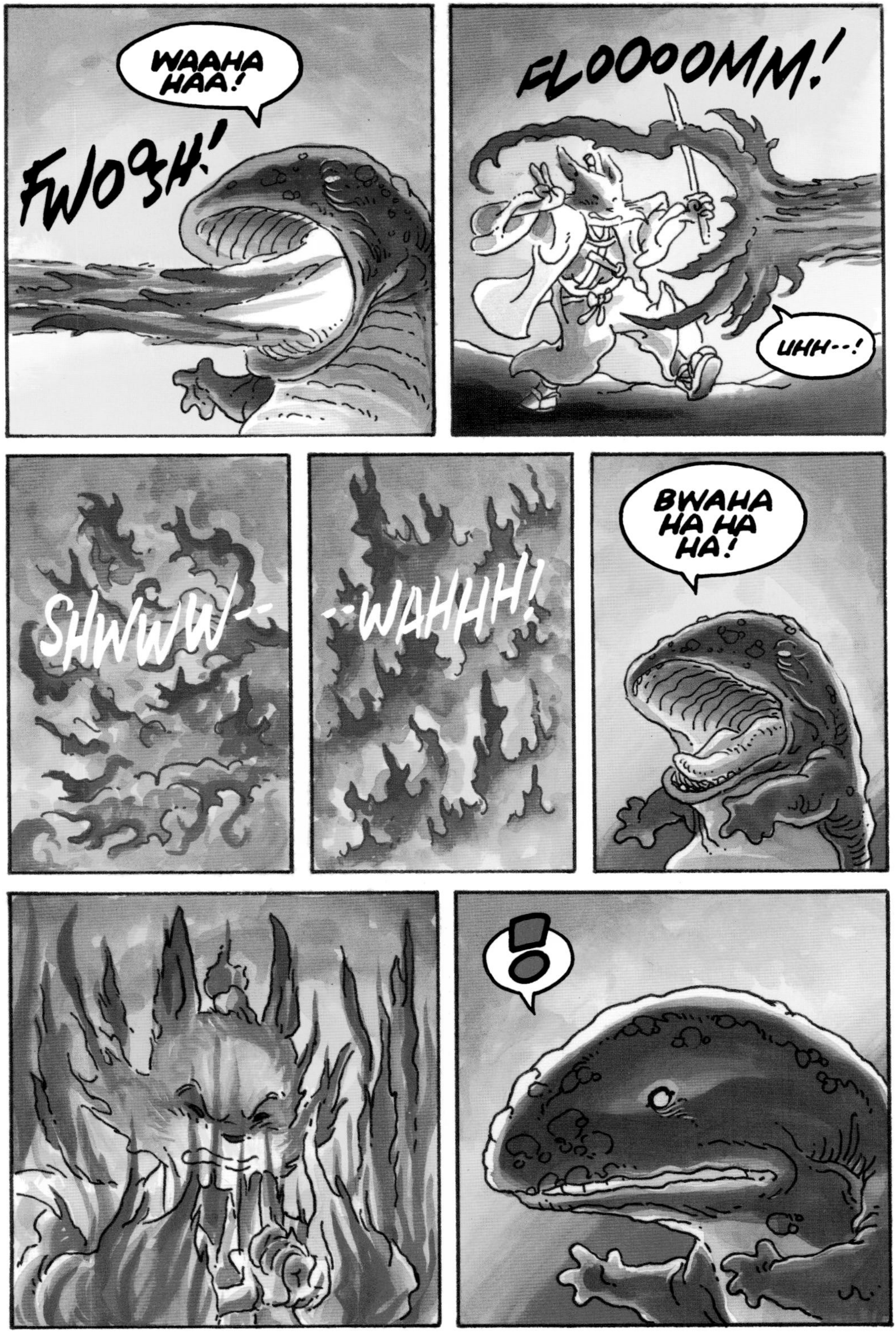
WAAHA HAA!
FWOOSH!
FLOOOOMM!
UHH--!
SHWWW--
--WAHHH!
BWAHA HA HA HA!
!?

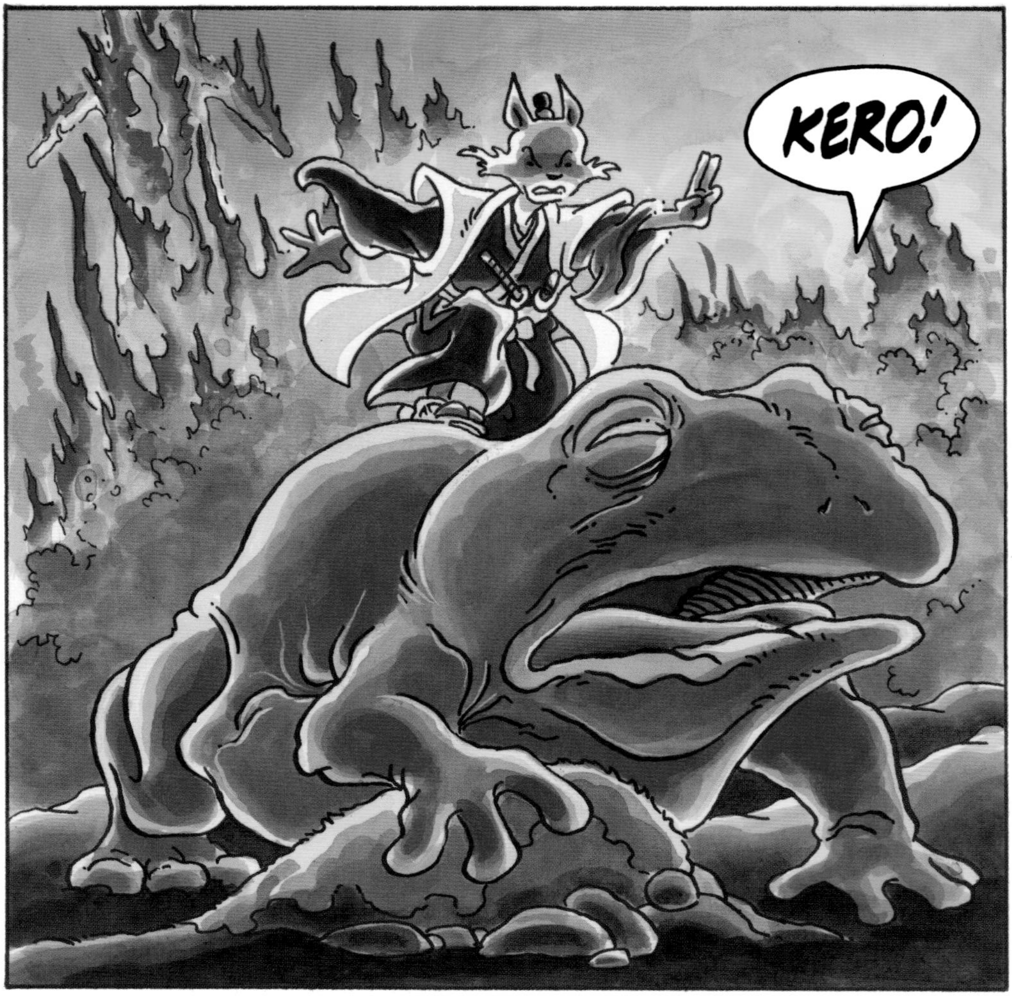
KERO!

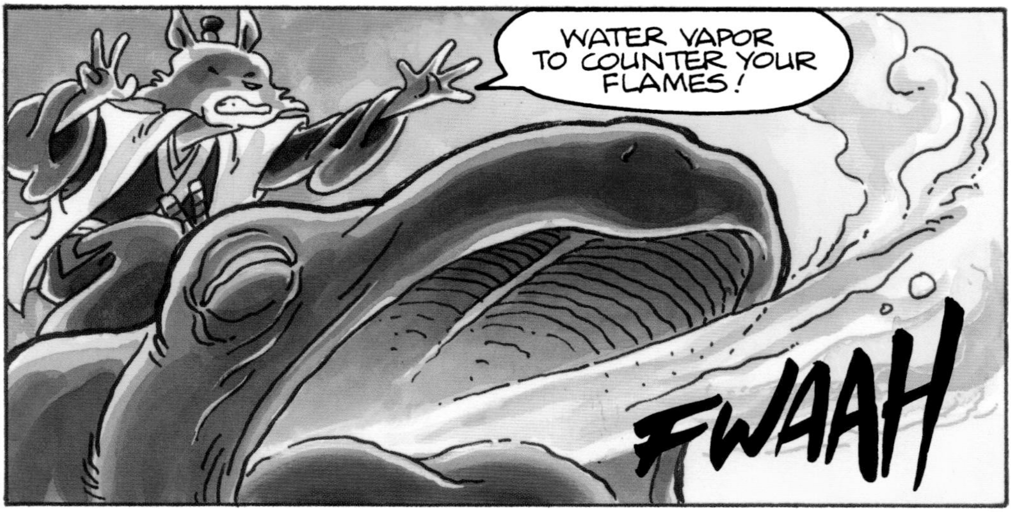
WATER VAPOR TO COUNTER YOUR FLAMES!
FWAAH

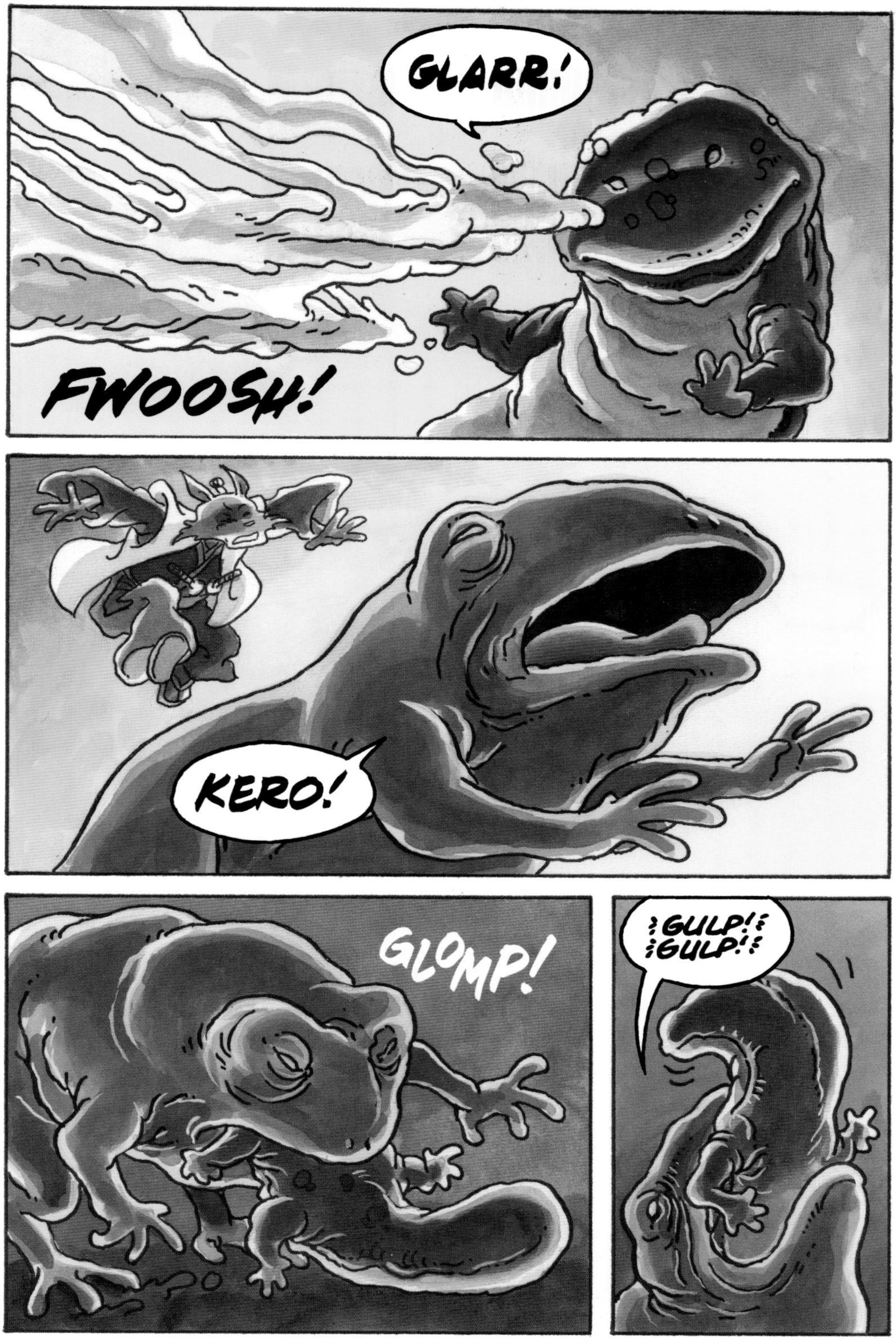
GLARR!
FWOOSH!
KERO!
GLOMP!
GULP!
GULP!

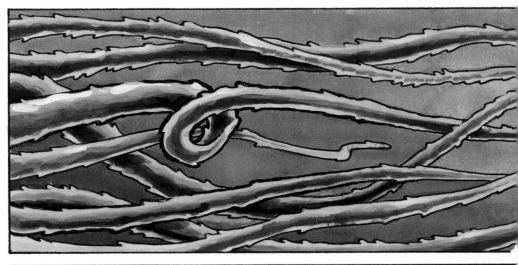

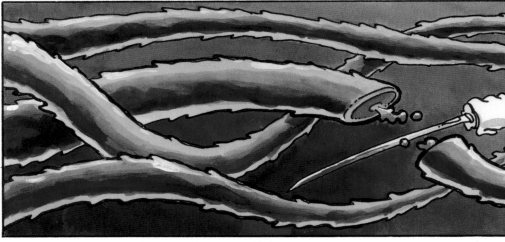

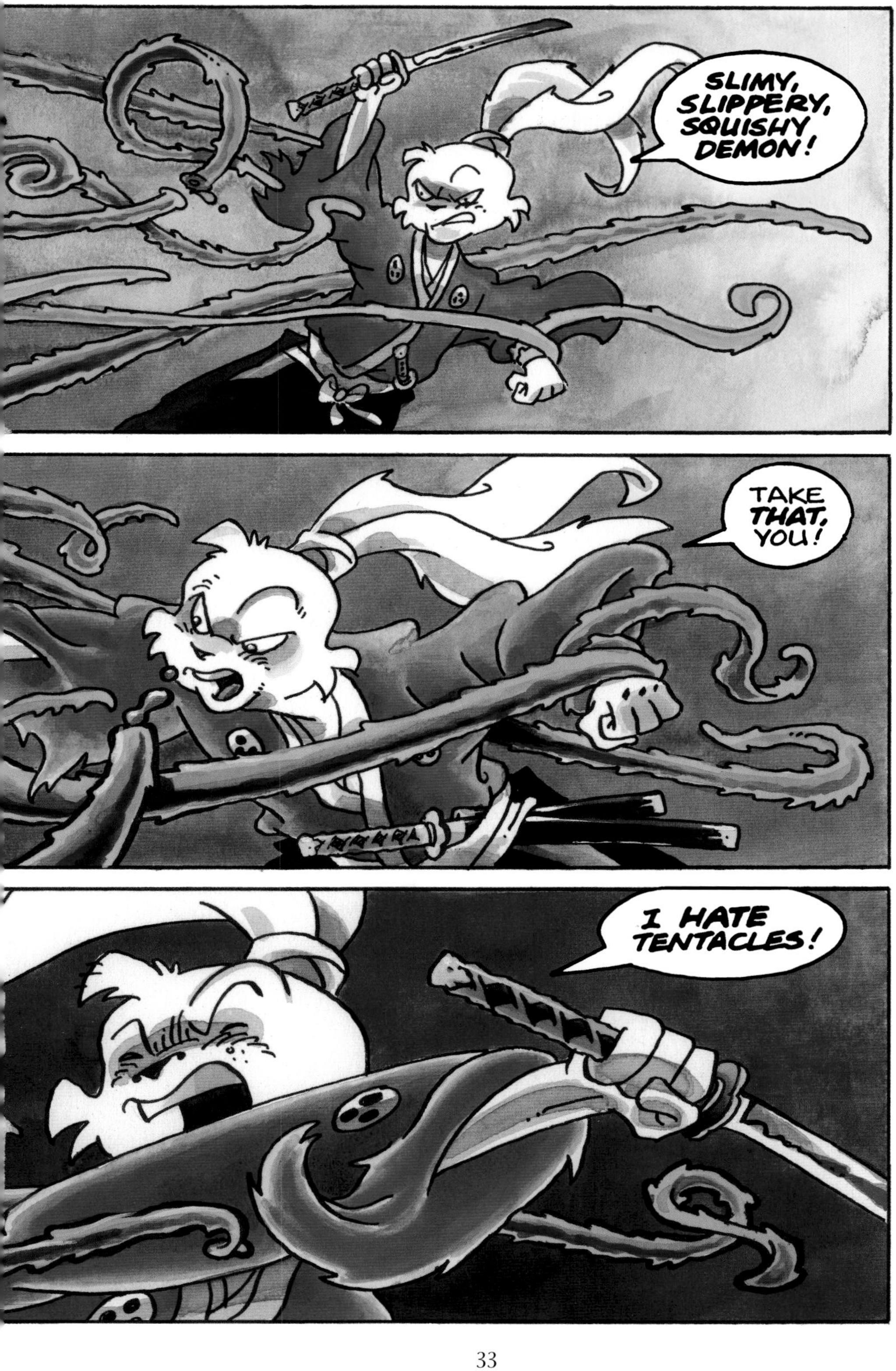
SLIMY, SLIPPERY, SQUISHY DEMON!
TAKE THAT, YOU!
I HATE TENTACLES!

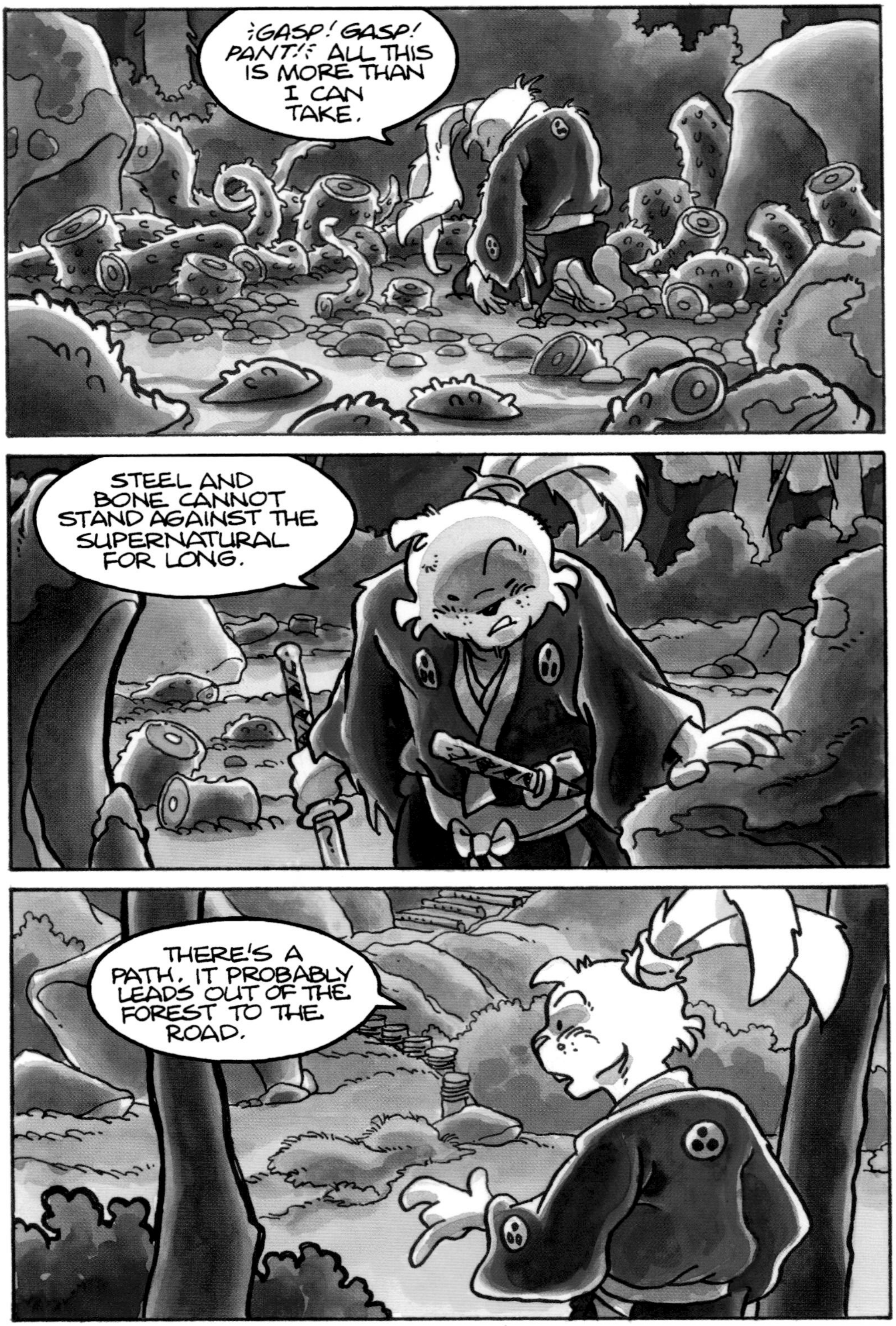
¡GASP! GASP! PANT!¡ ALL THIS IS MORE THAN I CAN TAKE.
STEEL AND BONE CANNOT STAND AGAINST THE SUPERNATURAL FOR LONG.
THERE'S A PATH. IT PROBABLY LEADS OUT OF THE FOREST TO THE ROAD.

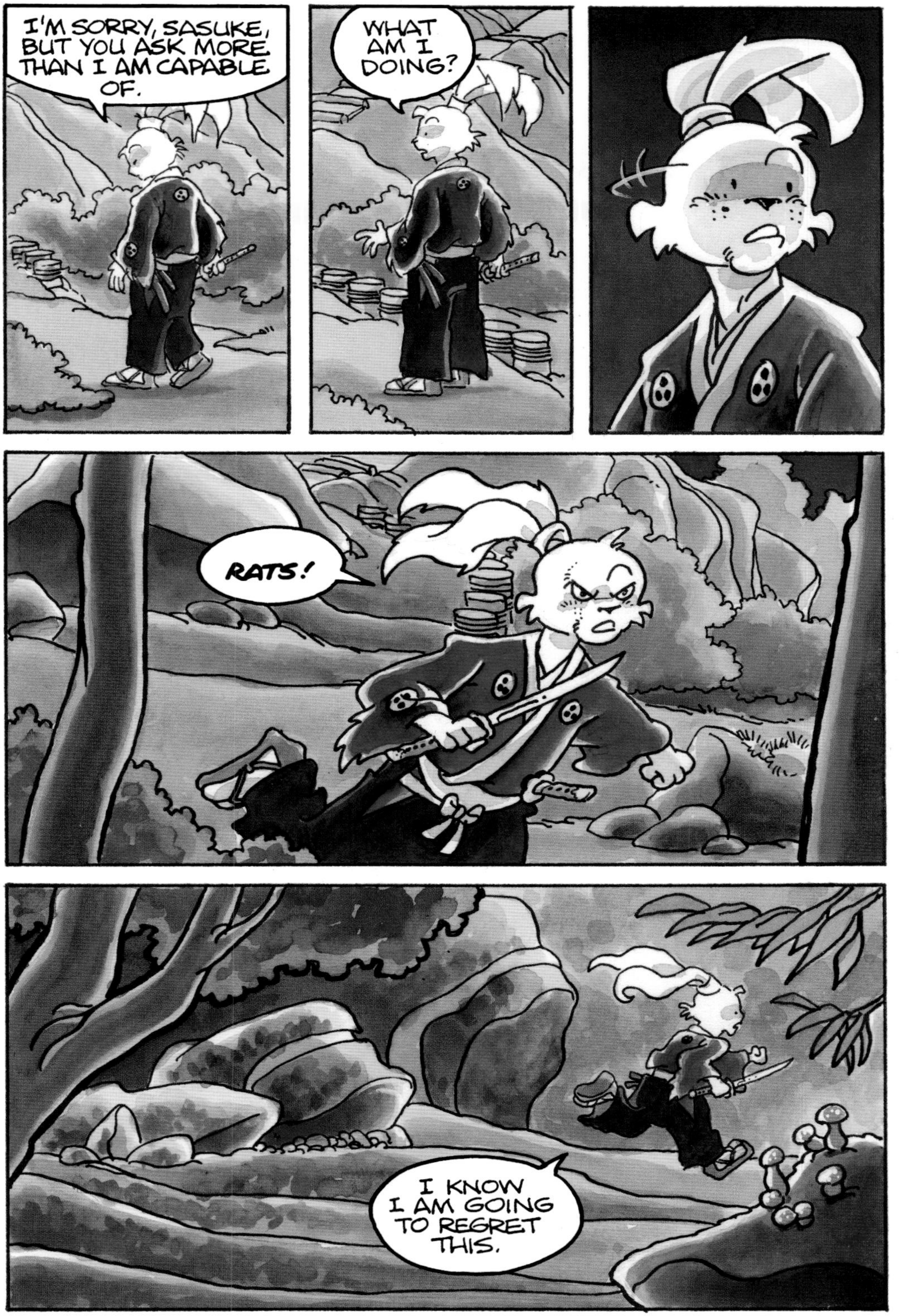
I'M SORRY, SASUKE, BUT YOU ASK MORE THAN I AM CAPABLE OF.
WHAT AM I DOING?
RATS!
I KNOW I AM GOING TO REGRET THIS.

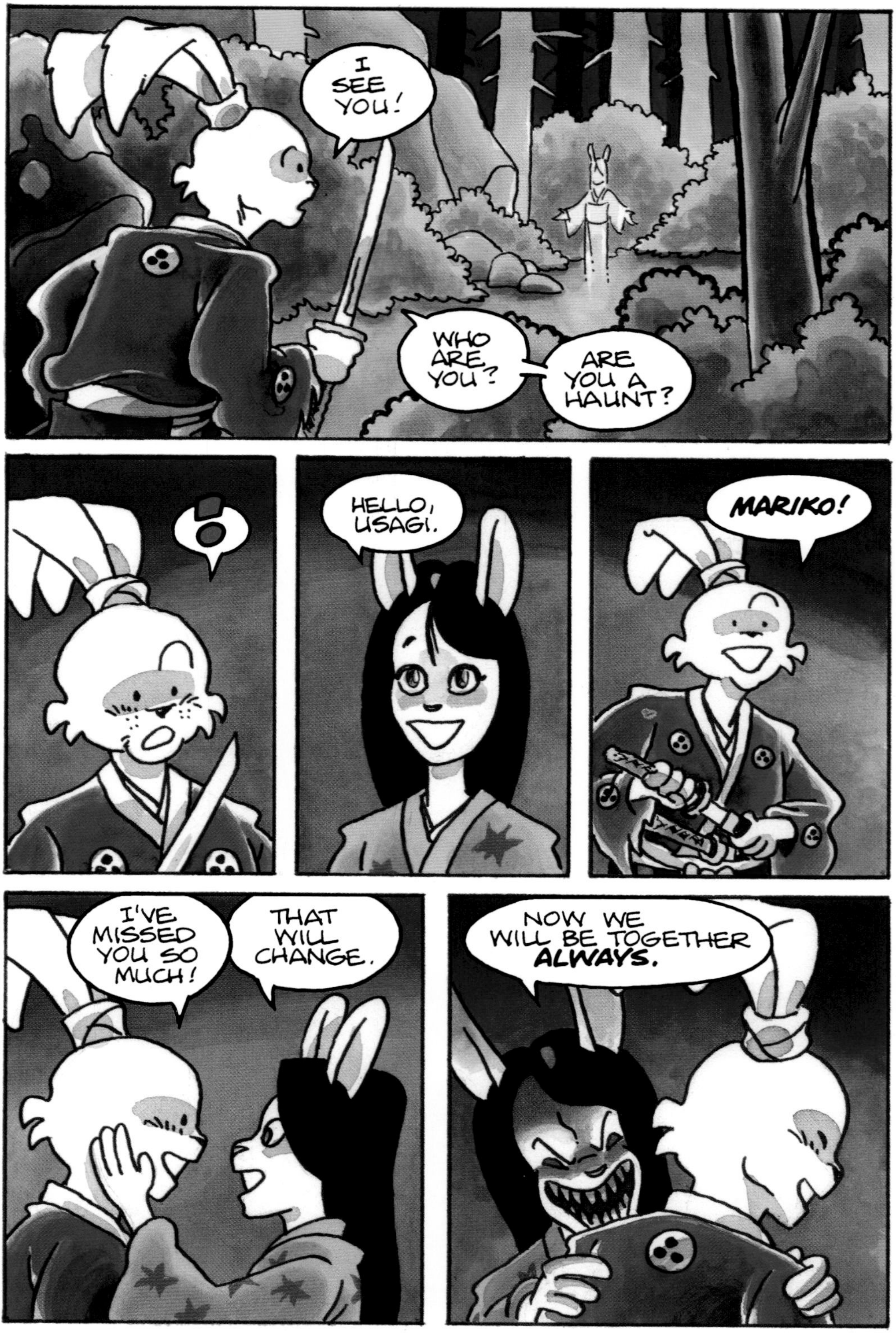
I SEE YOU!
WHO ARE YOU?
ARE YOU A HAUNT?
!
HELLO, USAGI.
MARIKO!
I'VE MISSED YOU SO MUCH!
THAT WILL CHANGE.
NOW WE WILL BE TOGETHER **ALWAYS.**

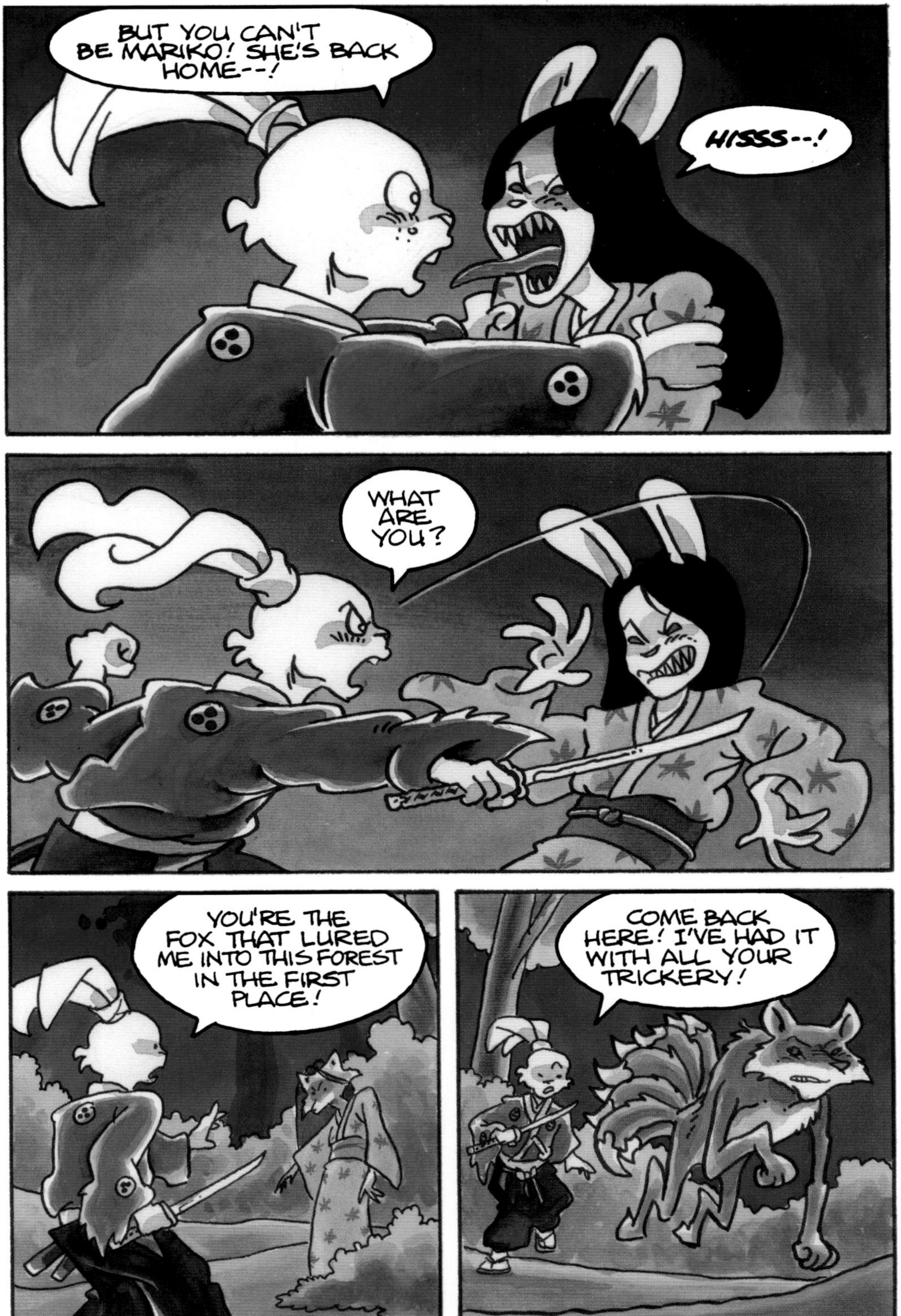
BUT YOU CAN'T BE MARIKO! SHE'S BACK HOME--!
HISSS--!
WHAT ARE YOU?
YOU'RE THE FOX THAT LURED ME INTO THIS FOREST IN THE FIRST PLACE!
COME BACK HERE! I'VE HAD IT WITH ALL YOUR TRICKERY!

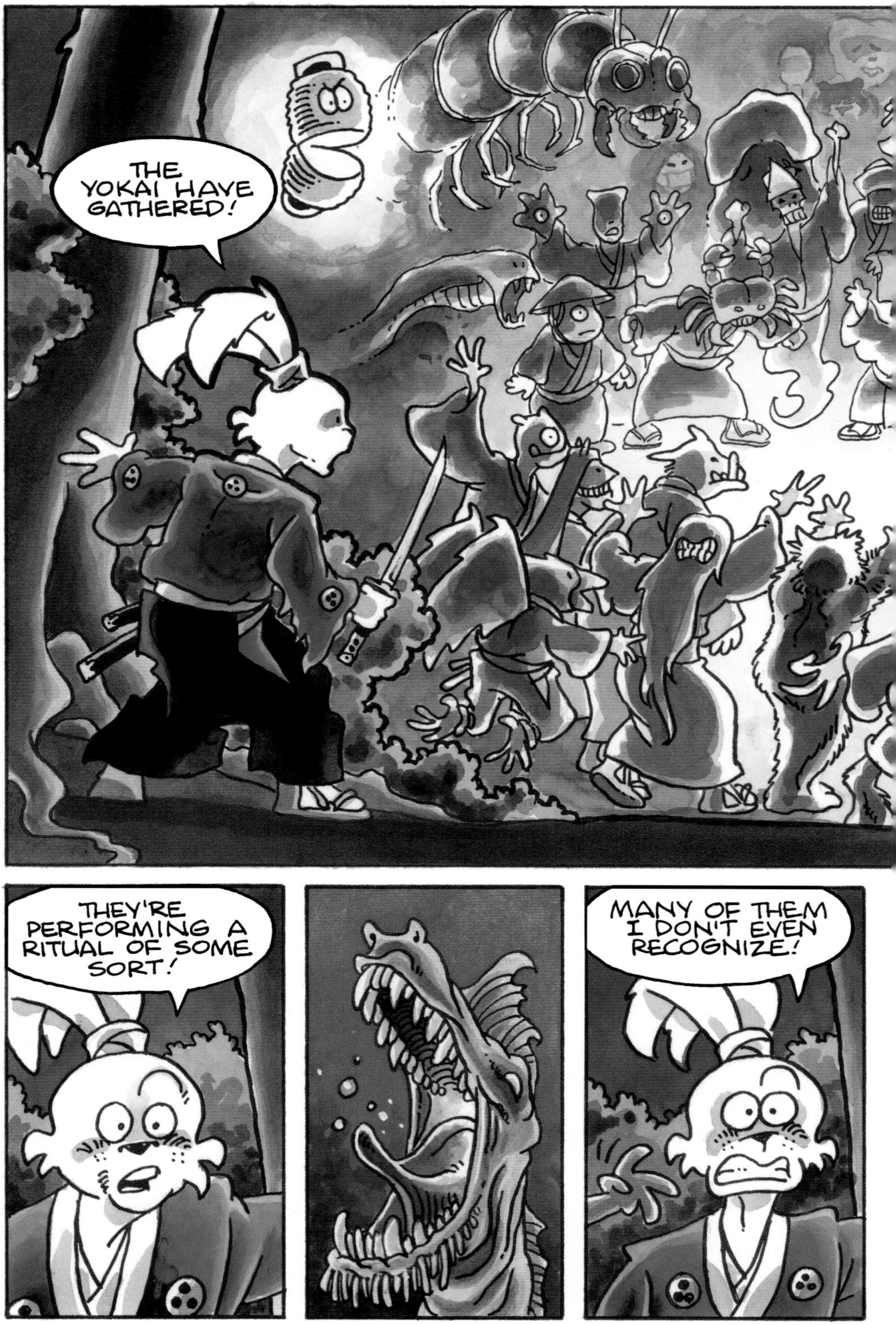
THE YOKAI HAVE GATHERED!
THEY'RE PERFORMING A RITUAL OF SOME SORT!
MANY OF THEM I DON'T EVEN RECOGNIZE!

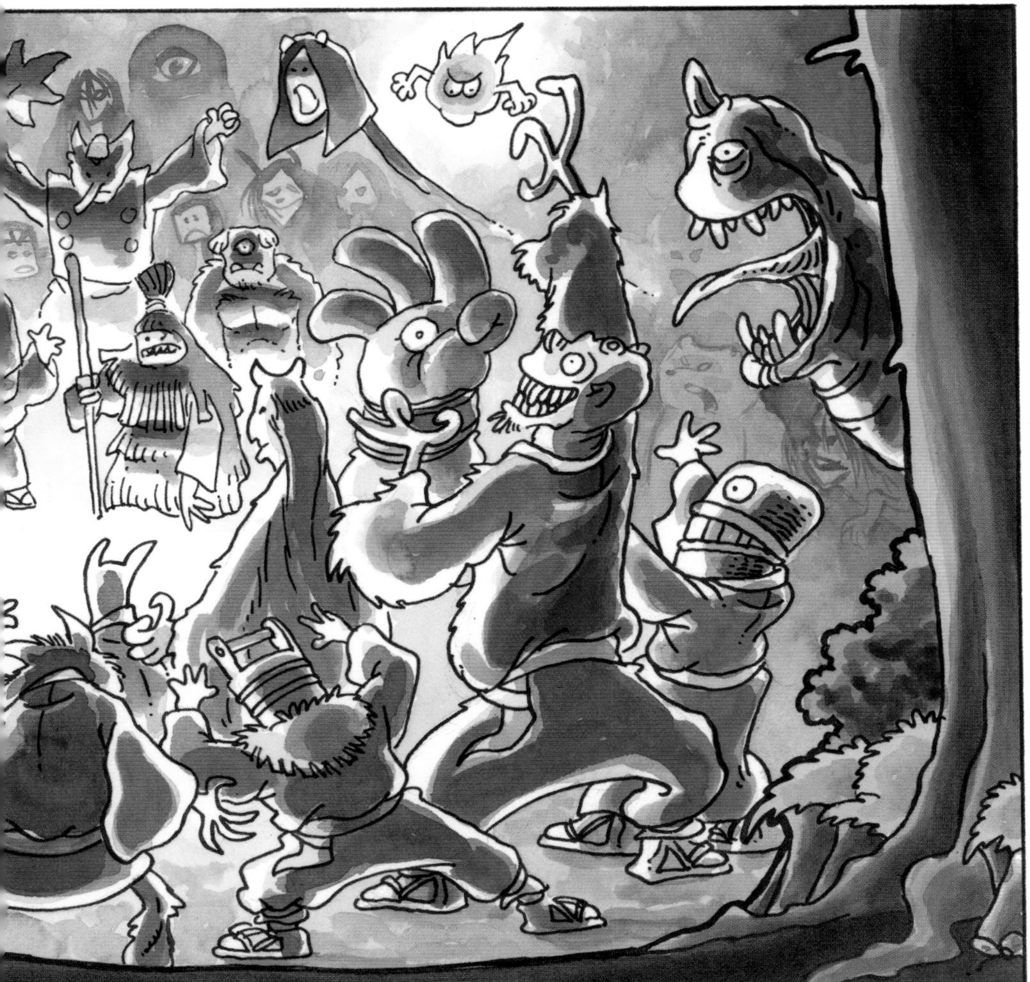
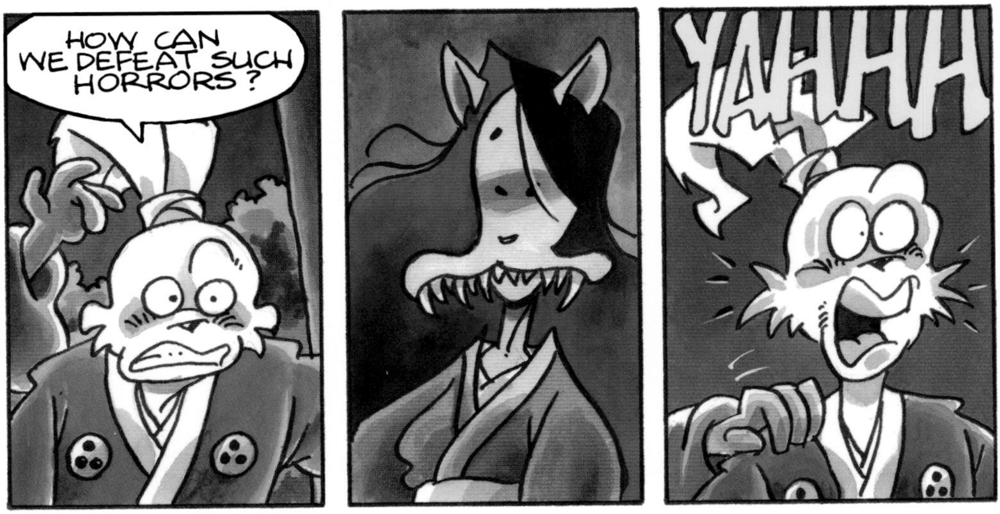
HOW CAN WE DEFEAT SUCH HORRORS?
YAHHH

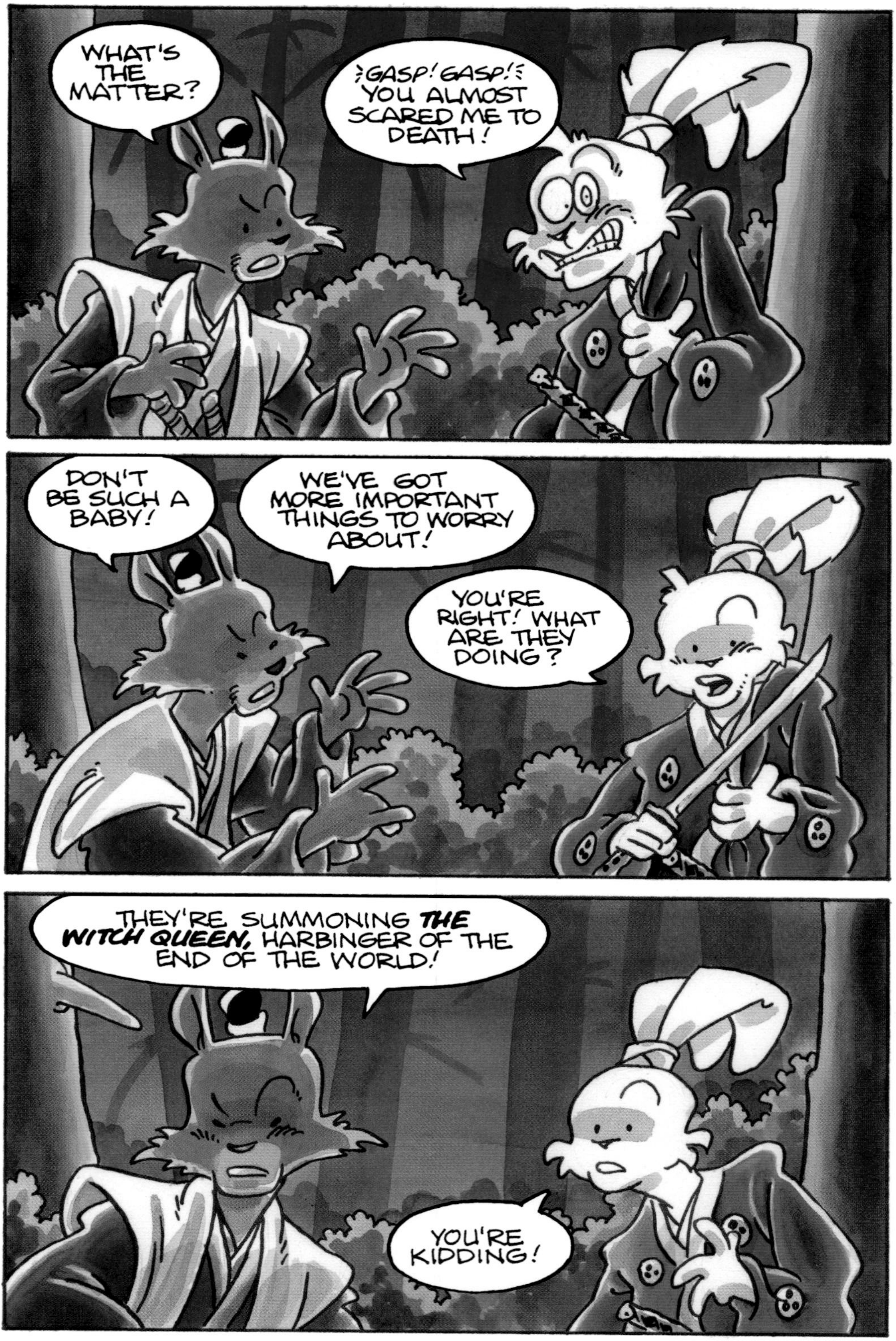
WHAT'S THE MATTER?
⁝GASP! GASP!⁝ YOU ALMOST SCARED ME TO DEATH!
DON'T BE SUCH A BABY!
WE'VE GOT MORE IMPORTANT THINGS TO WORRY ABOUT!
YOU'RE RIGHT! WHAT ARE THEY DOING?
THEY'RE SUMMONING **THE WITCH QUEEN,** HARBINGER OF THE END OF THE WORLD!
YOU'RE KIDDING!

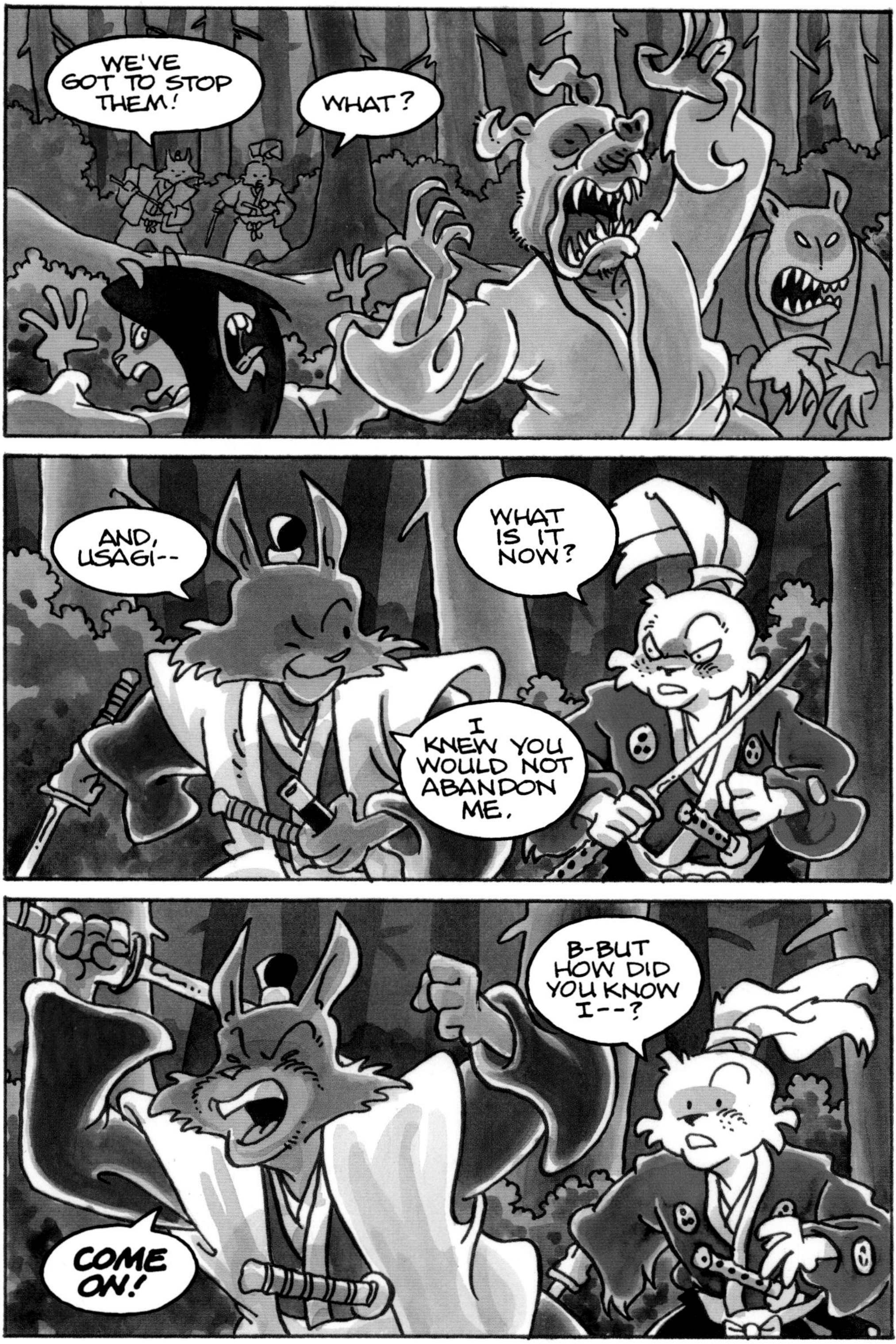
WE'VE GOT TO STOP THEM!
WHAT?
AND, USAGI--
WHAT IS IT NOW?
I KNEW YOU WOULD NOT ABANDON ME.
B-BUT HOW DID YOU KNOW I--?
COME ON!

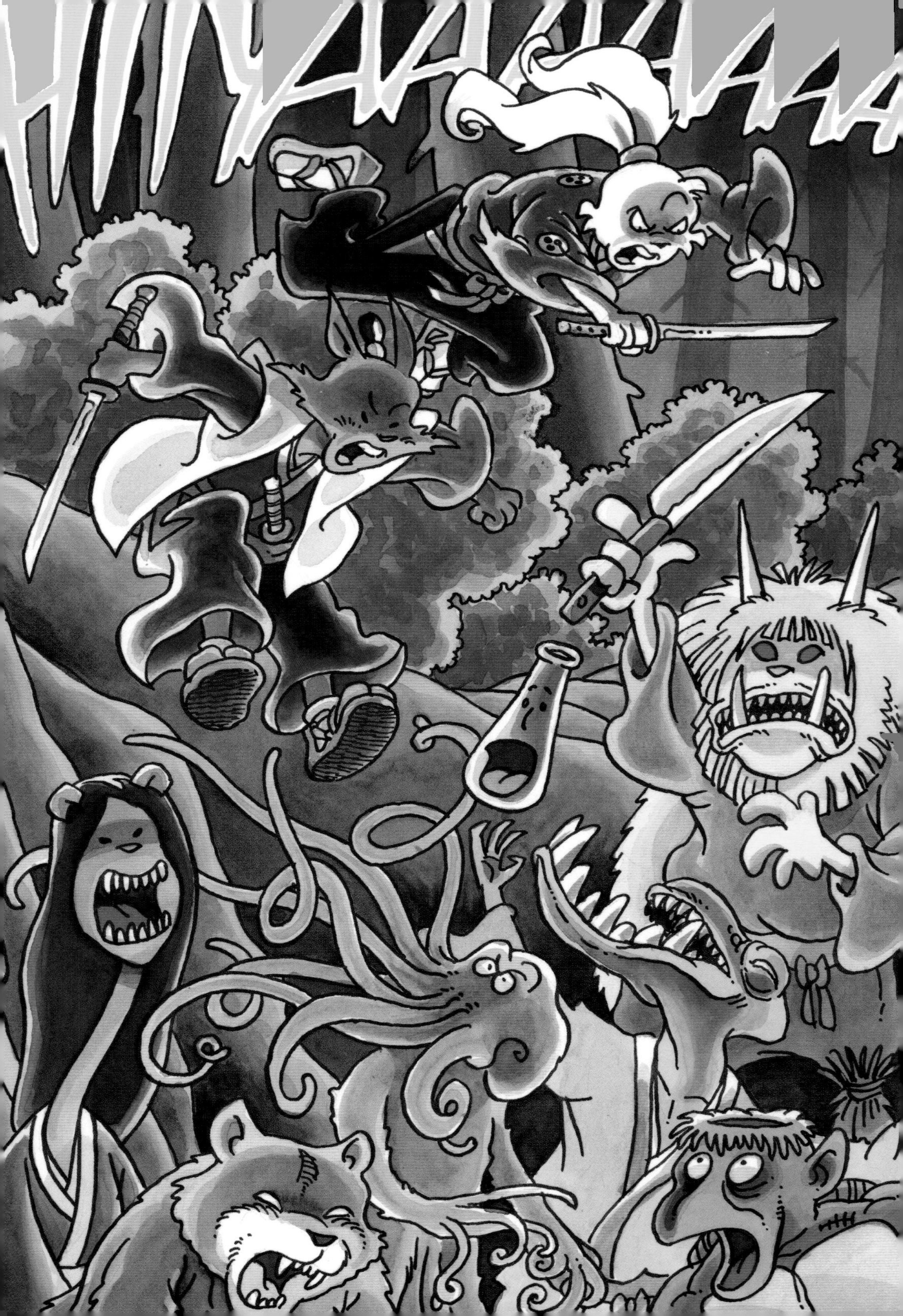
HIYAAAAAAA

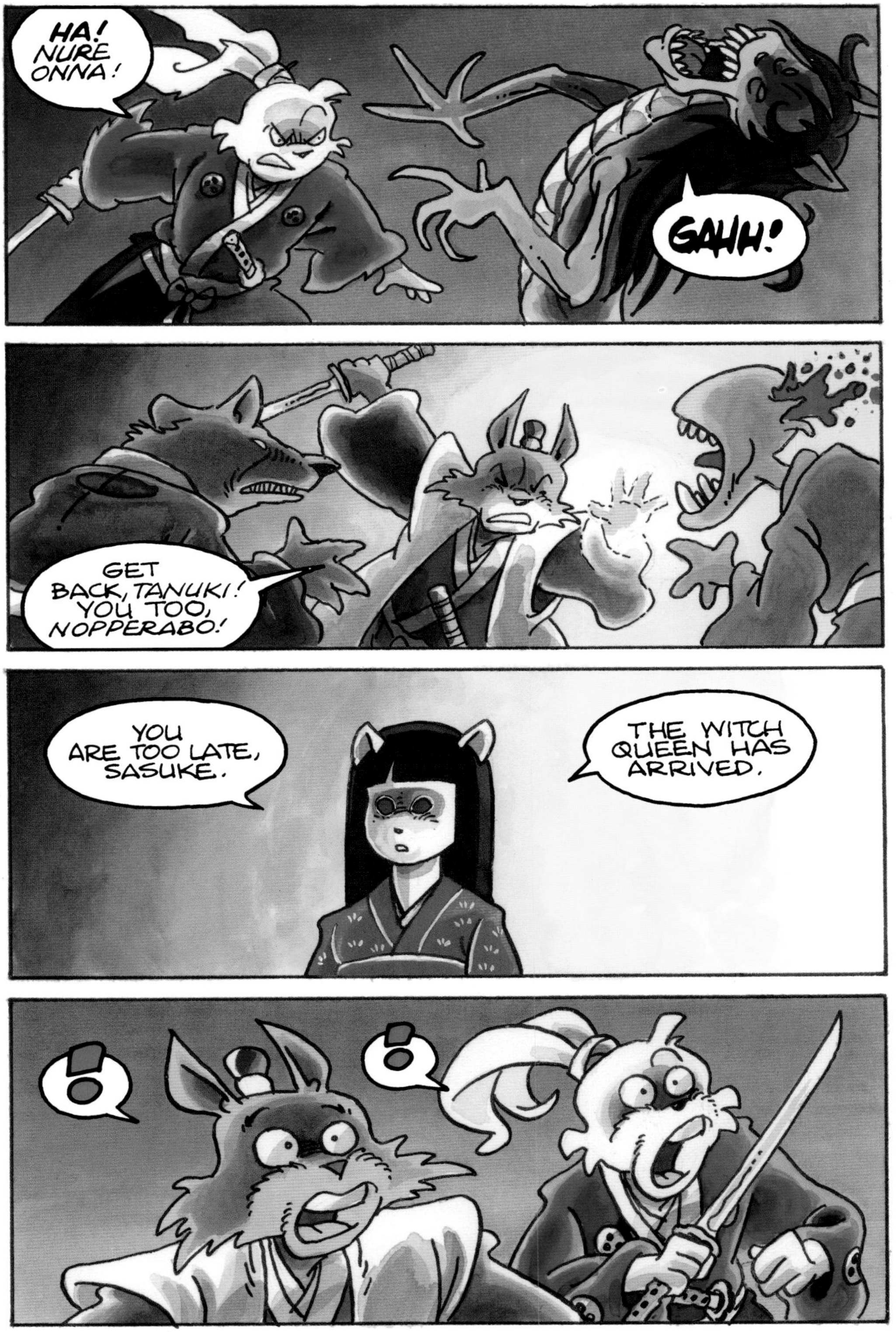
HA! NURE ONNA!
GAHH!
GET BACK, TANUKI! YOU TOO, NOPPERABO!
YOU ARE TOO LATE, SASUKE.
THE WITCH QUEEN HAS ARRIVED.
!
!

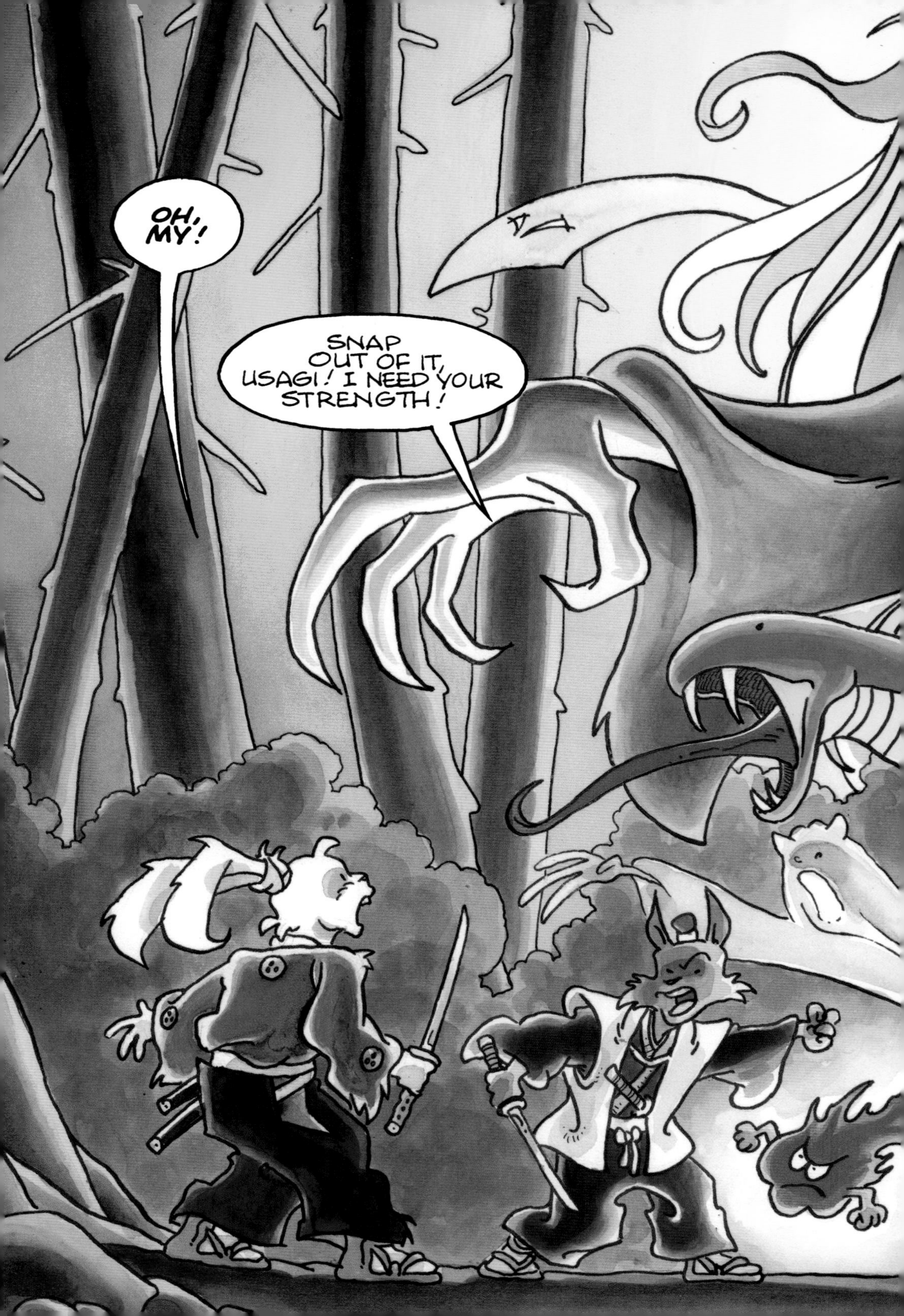
OH, MY!
SNAP OUT OF IT, USAGI! I NEED YOUR STRENGTH!

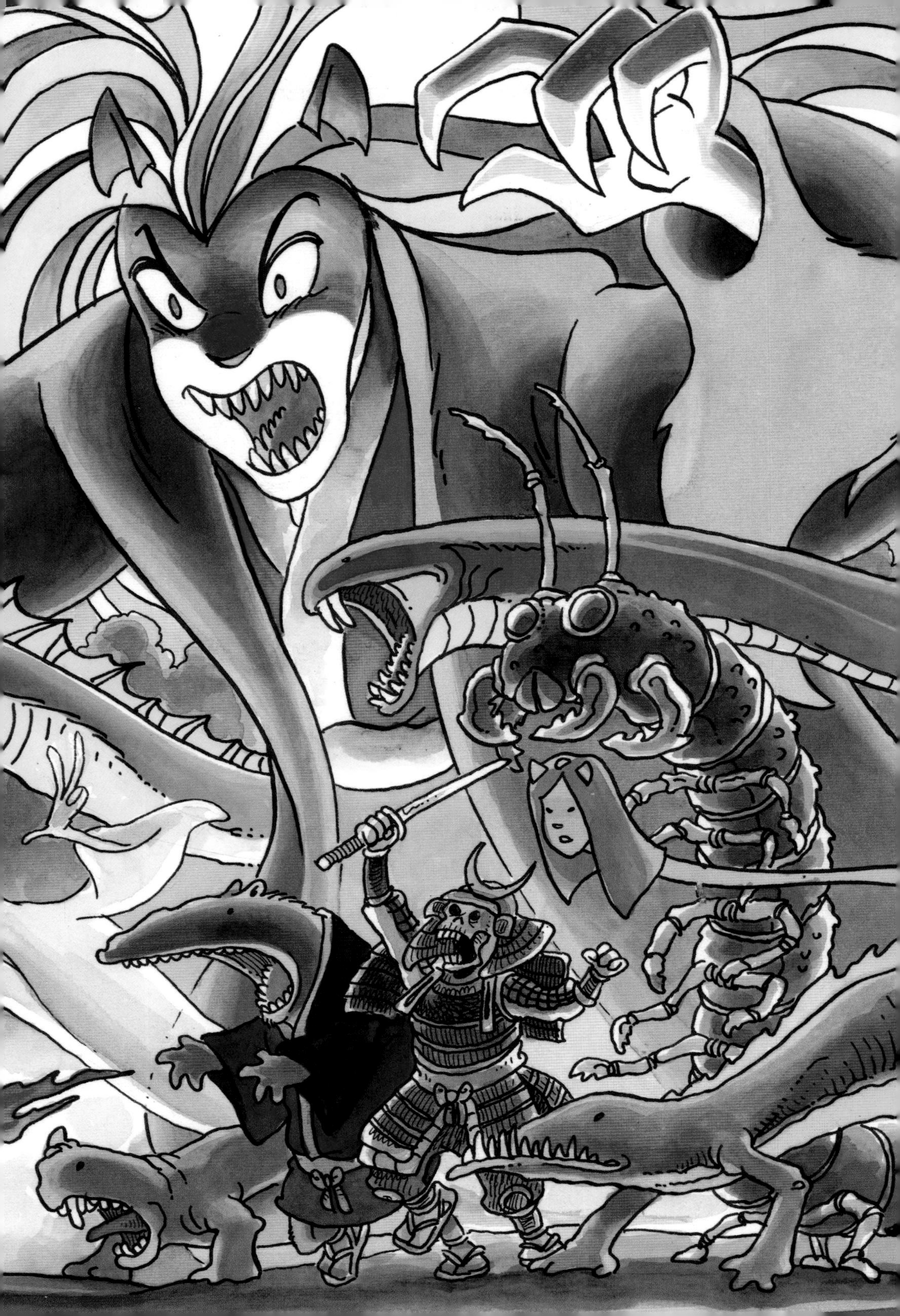

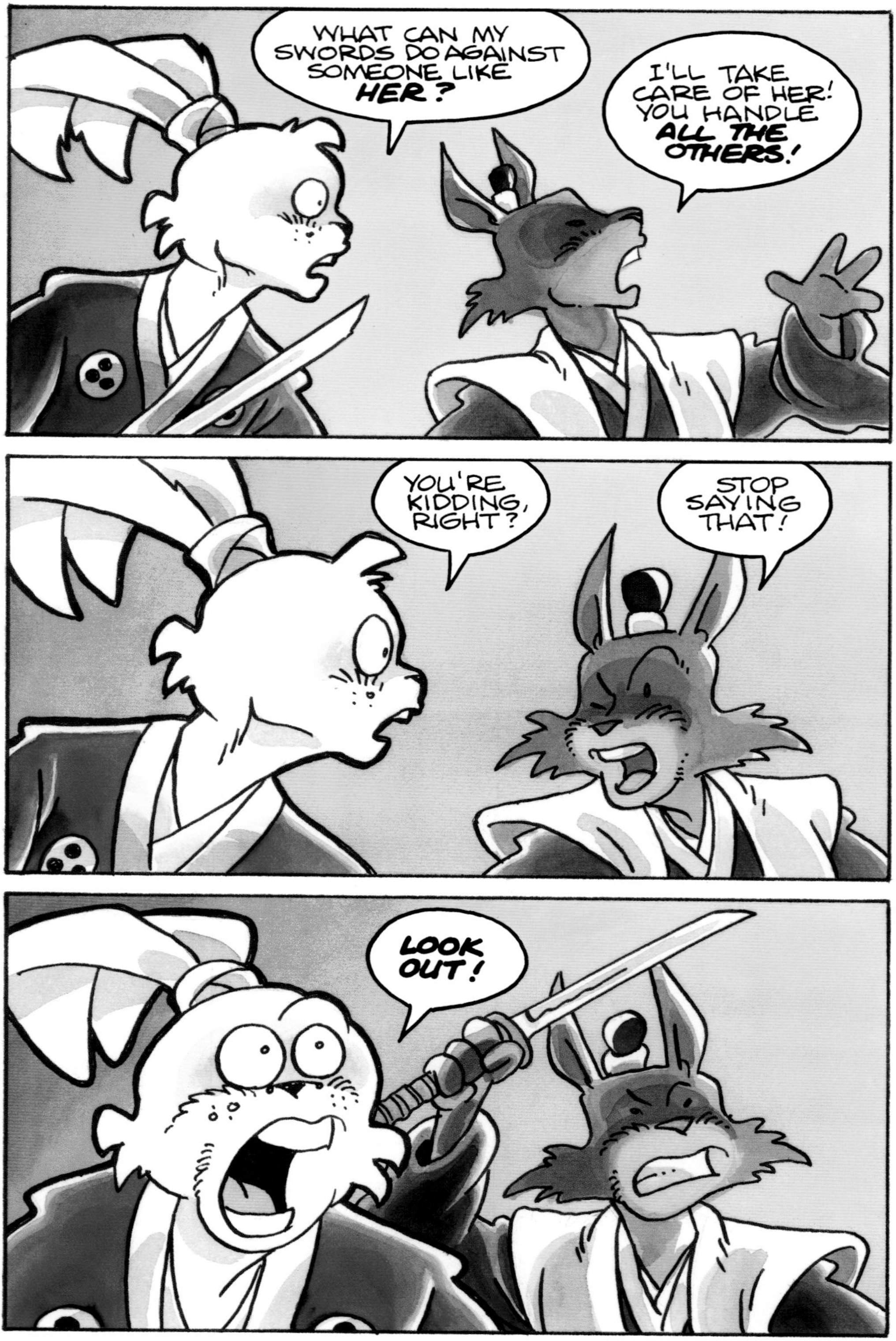
WHAT CAN MY SWORDS DO AGAINST SOMEONE LIKE **HER**?
I'LL TAKE CARE OF HER! YOU HANDLE **ALL THE OTHERS**!
YOU'RE KIDDING, RIGHT?
STOP SAYING THAT!
LOOK OUT!

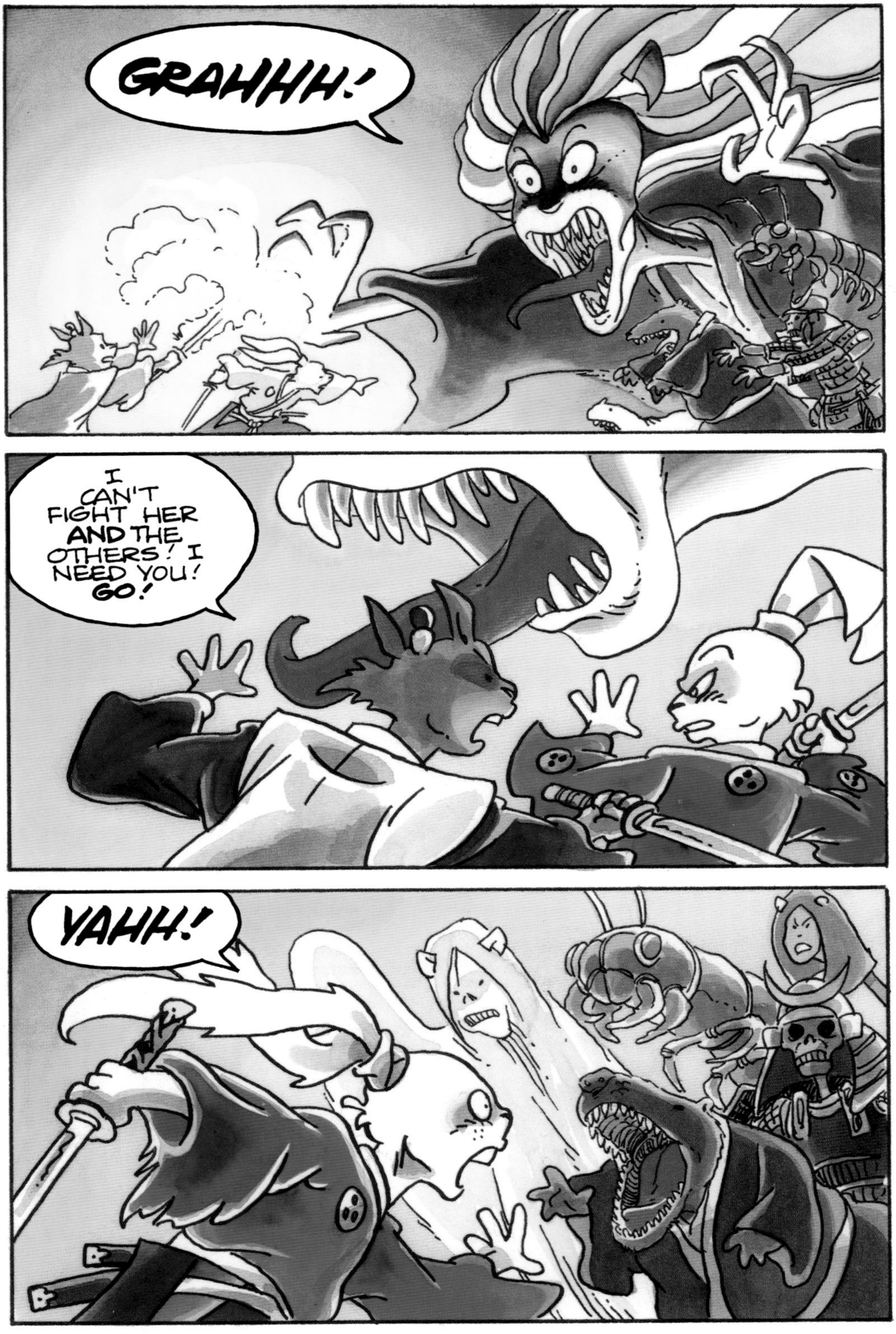
GRAHHH!
I CAN'T FIGHT HER AND THE OTHERS! I NEED YOU! GO!
YAHH!

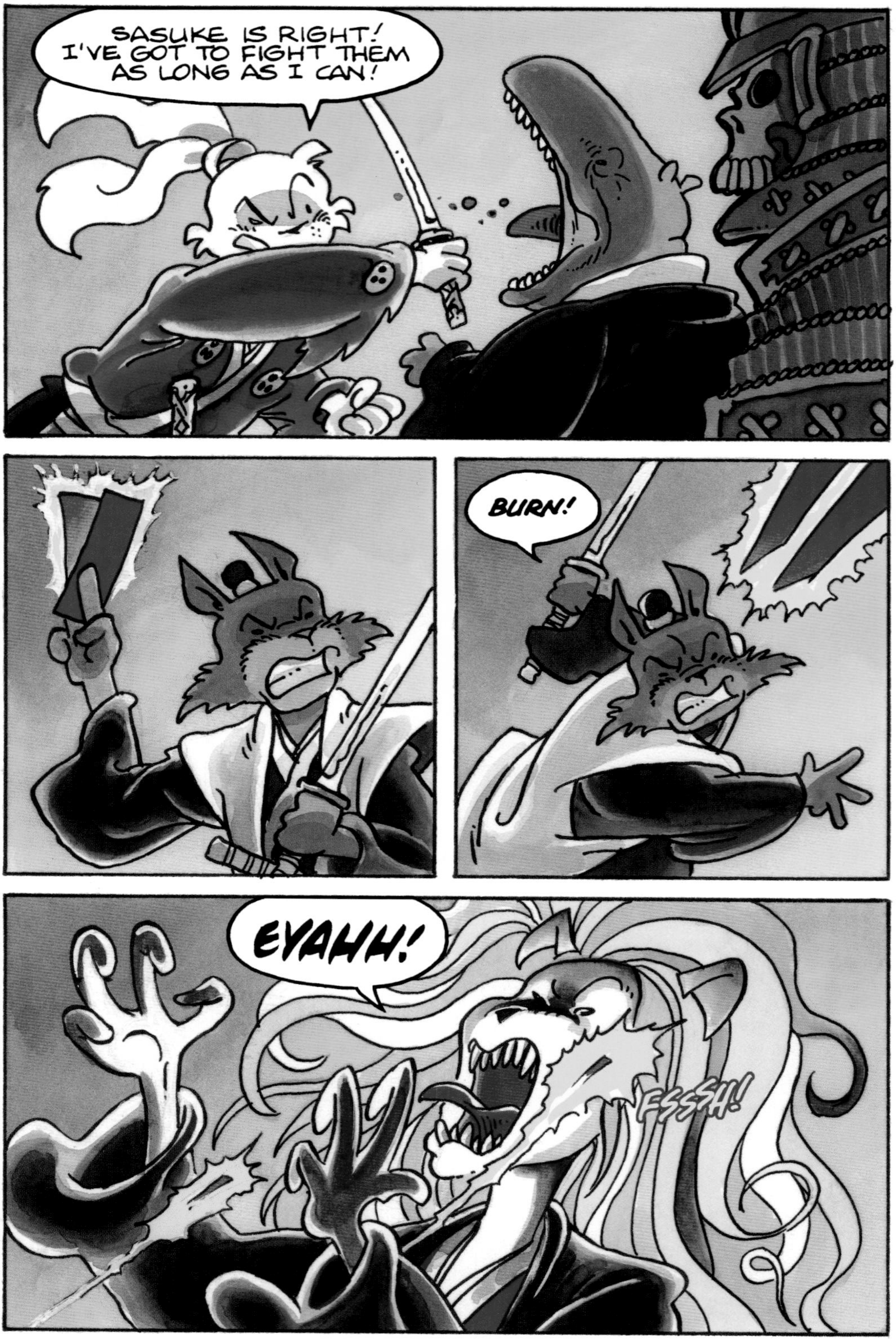
SASUKE IS RIGHT! I'VE GOT TO FIGHT THEM AS LONG AS I CAN!
BURN!
EYAHH!
FSSSH!

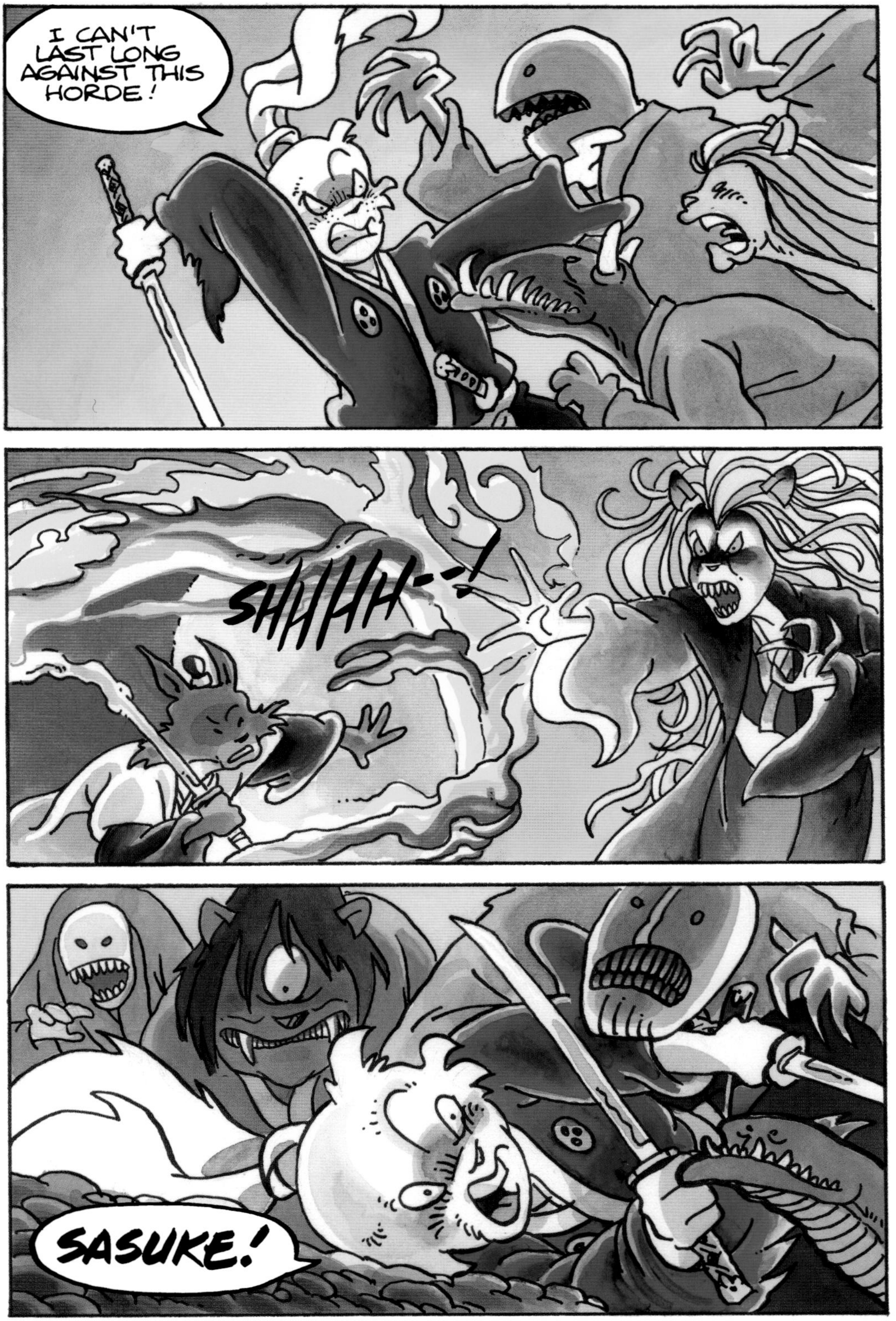
I CAN'T LAST LONG AGAINST THIS HORDE!
SHHHHH--!
SASUKE!

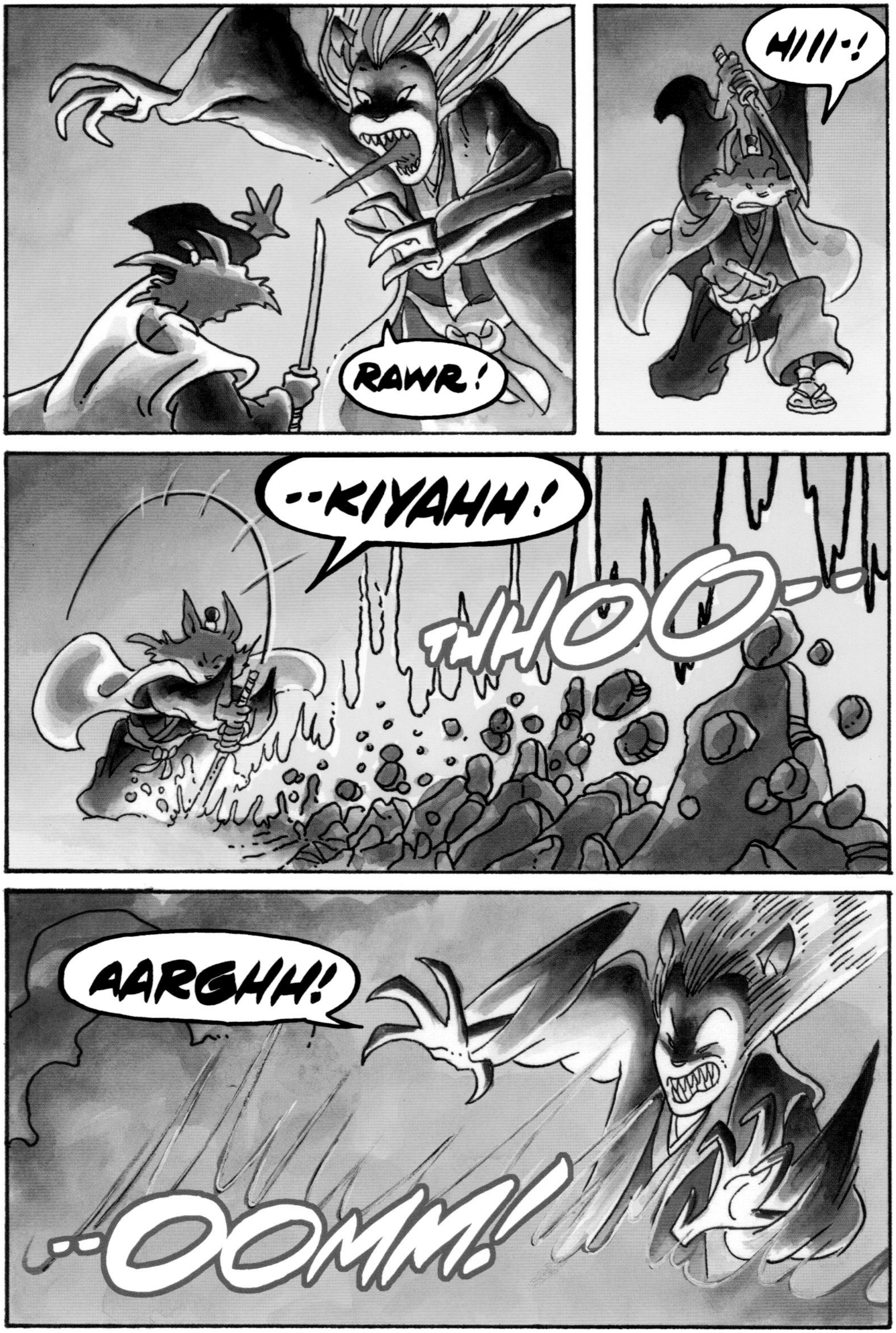
RAWR!
HIII--!
--KIYAHH!
THHOO---
AARGHH!
--OOMM!

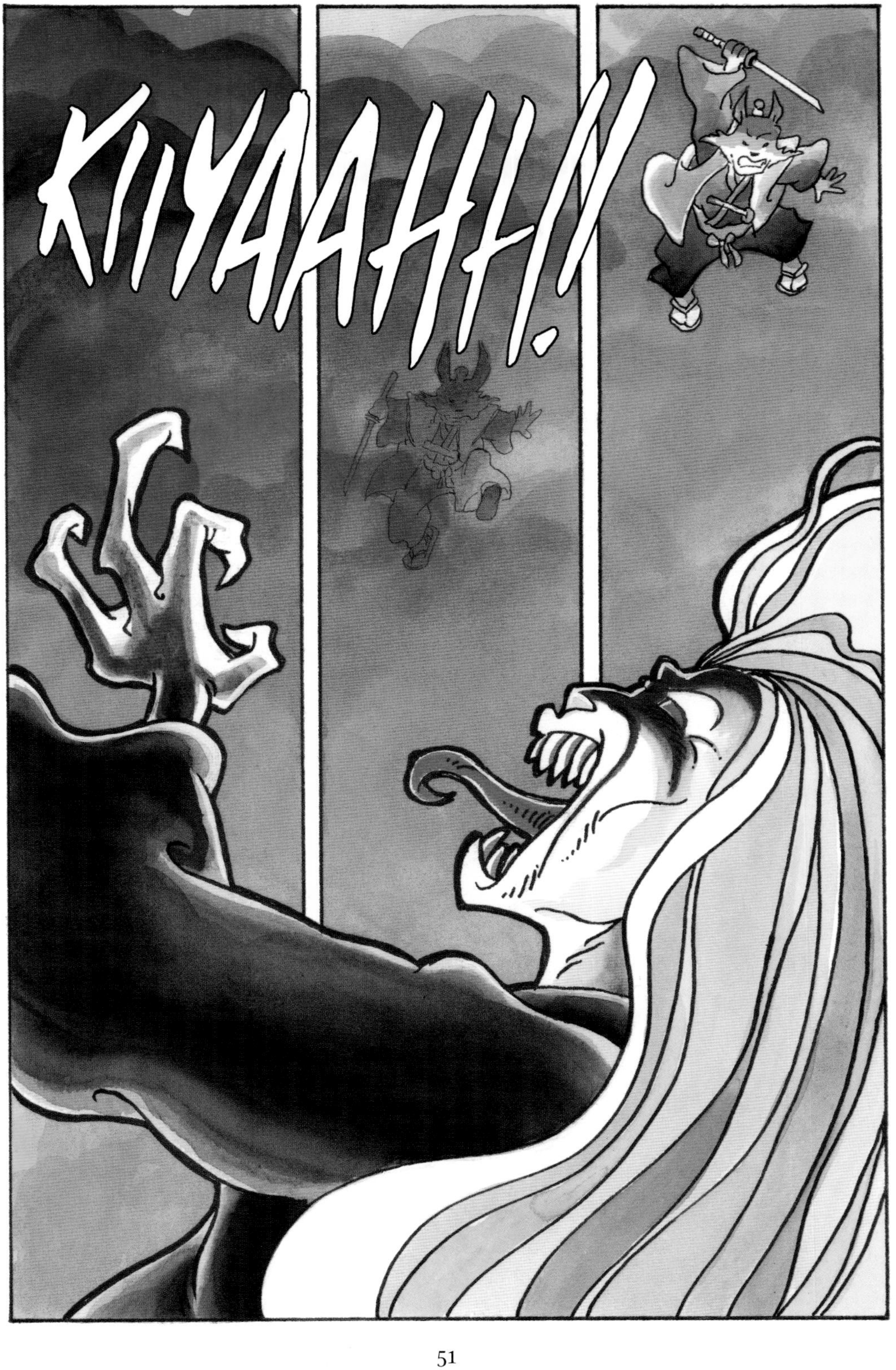
KIIYAAHH!!

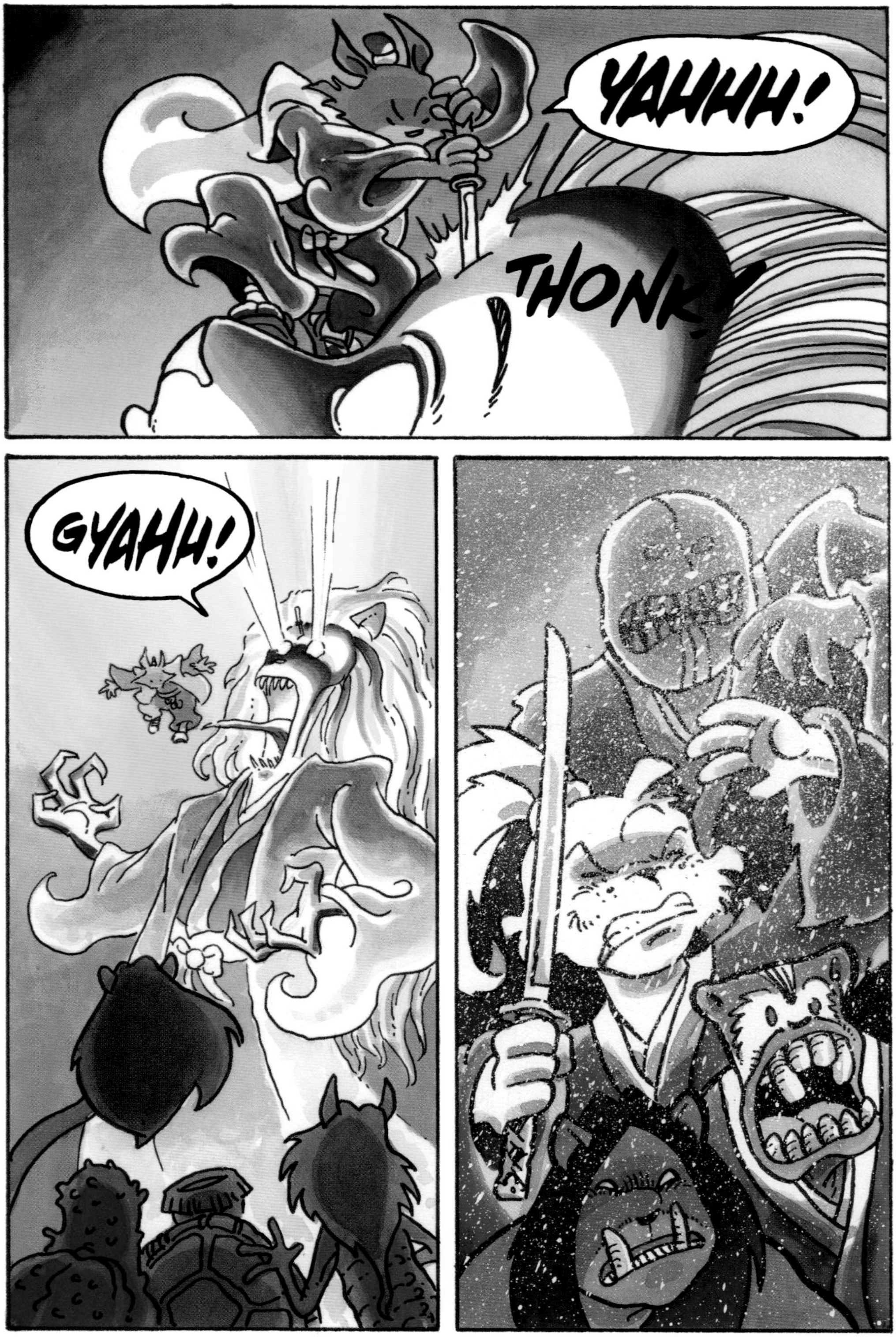
YAHHH!
THONK!
GYAHH!

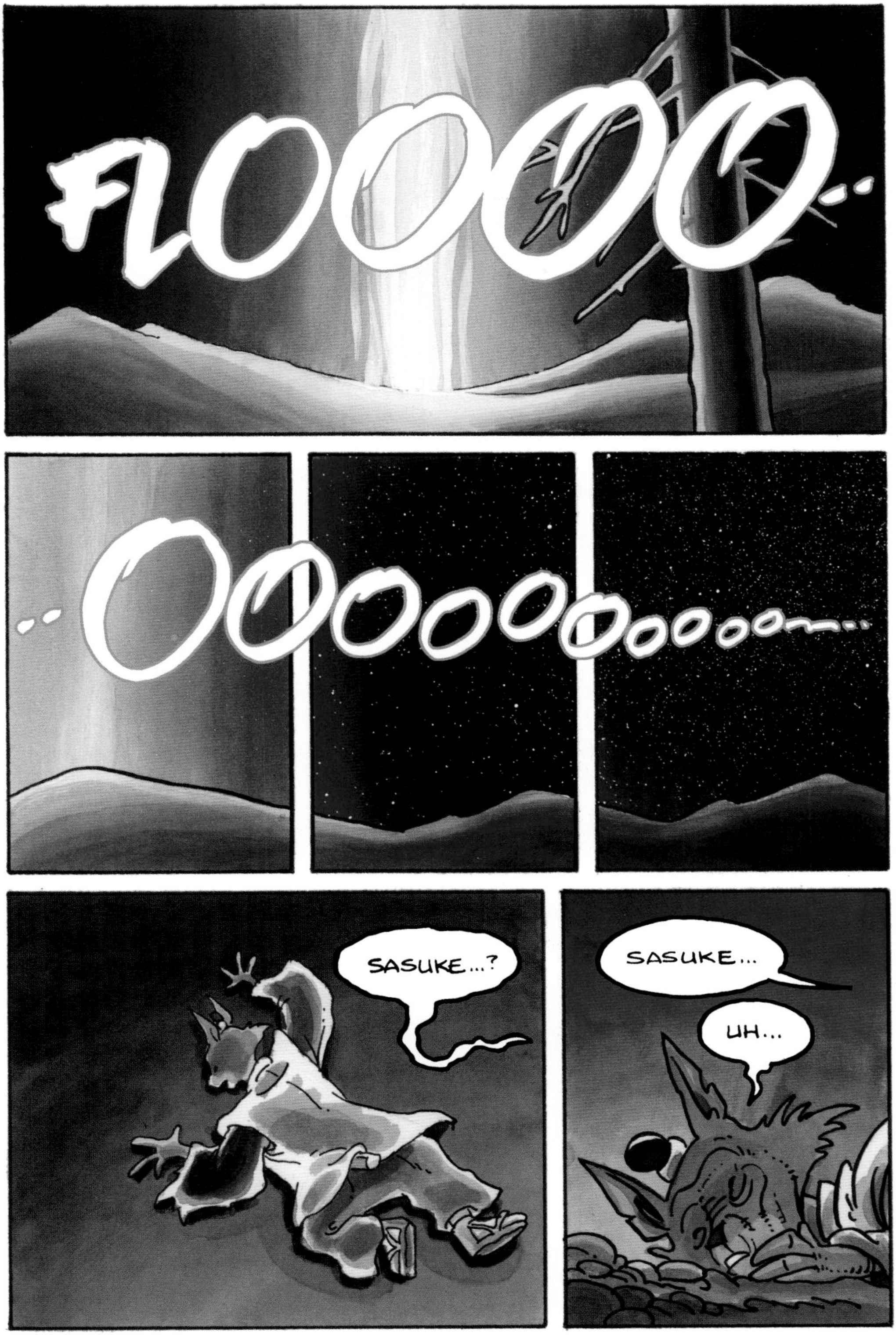
FLOOOOO..
..OOOOOOOOooooo...
SASUKE...?
SASUKE...
UH...

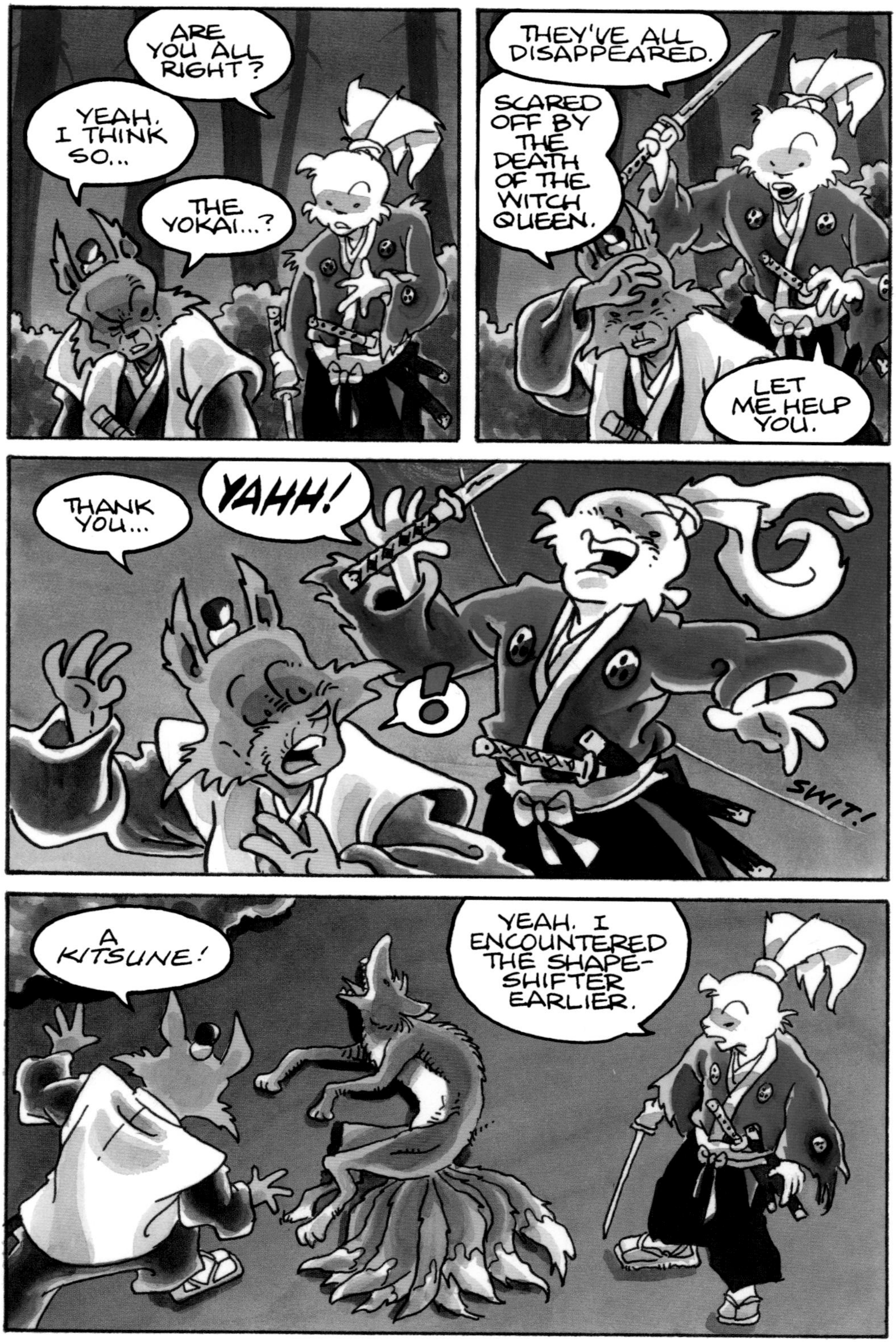

ARE YOU ALL RIGHT?
YEAH. I THINK SO...
THE YOKAI...?
THEY'VE ALL DISAPPEARED.
SCARED OFF BY THE DEATH OF THE WITCH QUEEN.
LET ME HELP YOU.
THANK YOU...
YAHH!
!
SWIT!
A KITSUNE!
YEAH. I ENCOUNTERED THE SHAPE-SHIFTER EARLIER.

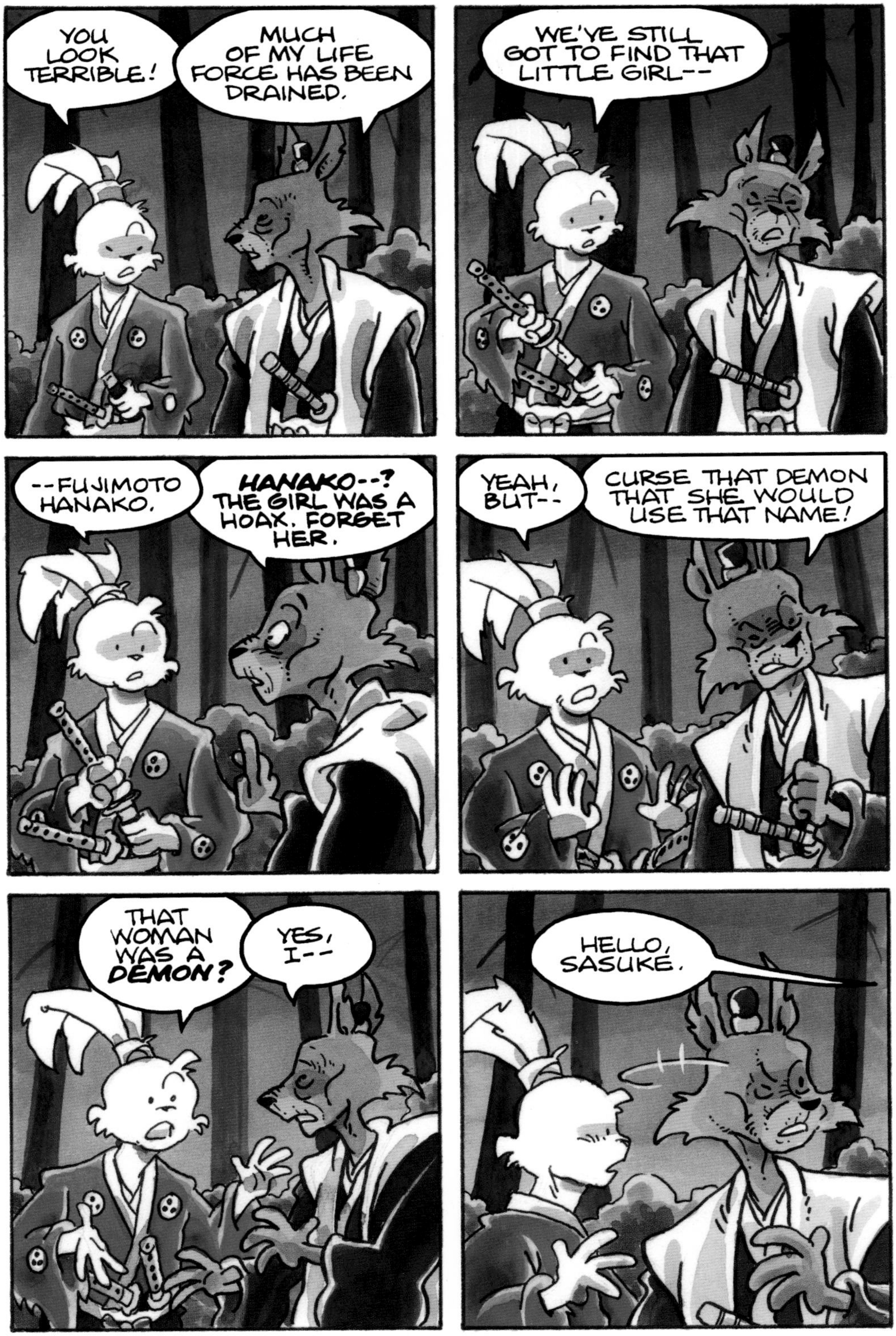
YOU LOOK TERRIBLE!
MUCH OF MY LIFE FORCE HAS BEEN DRAINED.
WE'VE STILL GOT TO FIND THAT LITTLE GIRL--
--FUJIMOTO HANAKO.
HANAKO--? THE GIRL WAS A HOAX. FORGET HER.
YEAH, BUT--
CURSE THAT DEMON THAT SHE WOULD USE THAT NAME!
THAT WOMAN WAS A DEMON?
YES, I--
HELLO, SASUKE.

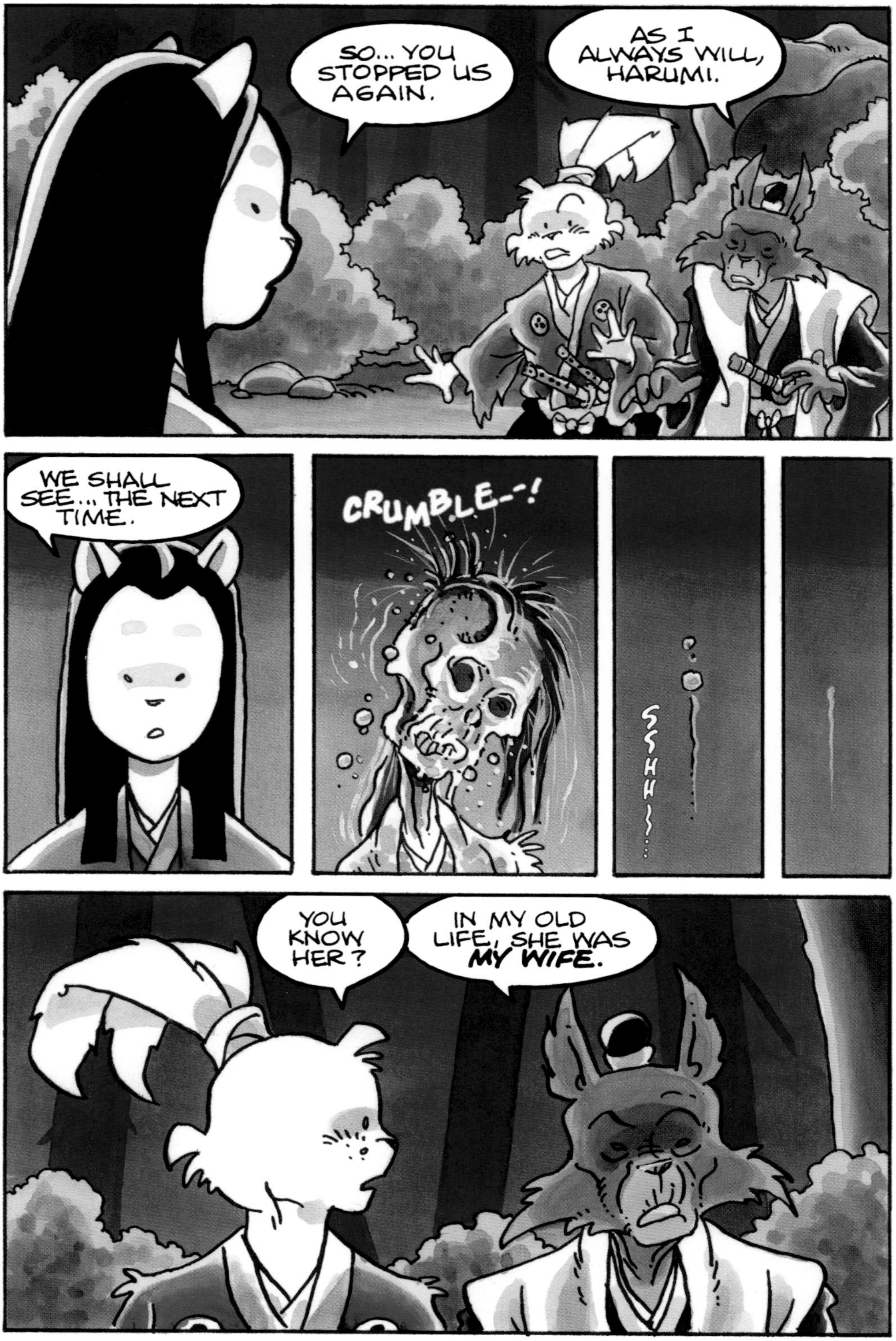
SO... YOU STOPPED US AGAIN.
AS I ALWAYS WILL, HARUMI.
WE SHALL SEE... THE NEXT TIME.
CRUMBLE--!
SSHHH...
YOU KNOW HER?
IN MY OLD LIFE, SHE WAS **MY WIFE.**

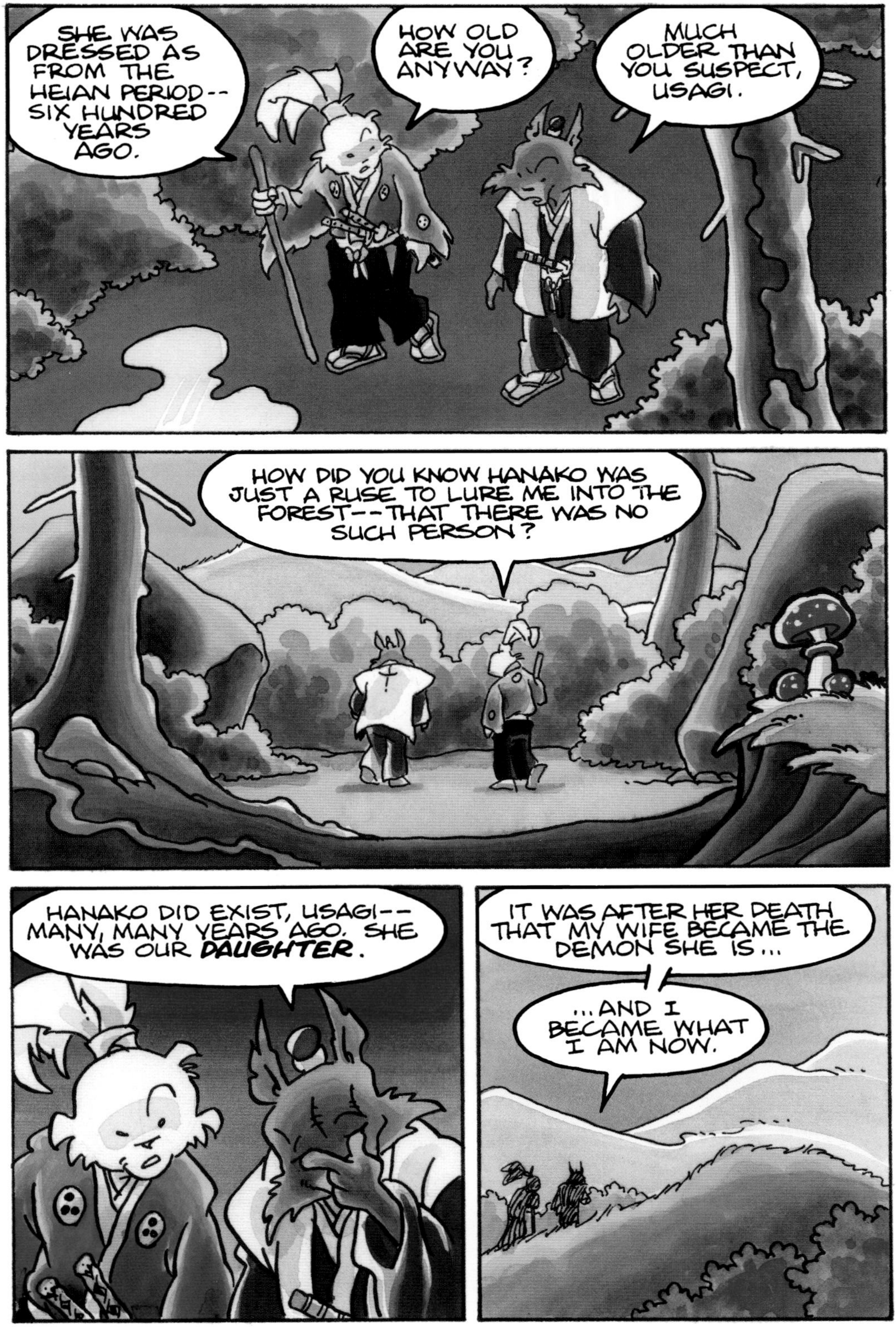
SHE WAS DRESSED AS FROM THE HEIAN PERIOD--SIX HUNDRED YEARS AGO.
HOW OLD ARE YOU ANYWAY?
MUCH OLDER THAN YOU SUSPECT, USAGI.
HOW DID YOU KNOW HANAKO WAS JUST A RUSE TO LURE ME INTO THE FOREST--THAT THERE WAS NO SUCH PERSON?
HANAKO DID EXIST, USAGI--MANY, MANY YEARS AGO. SHE WAS OUR DAUGHTER.
IT WAS AFTER HER DEATH THAT MY WIFE BECAME THE DEMON SHE IS...
...AND I BECAME WHAT I AM NOW.

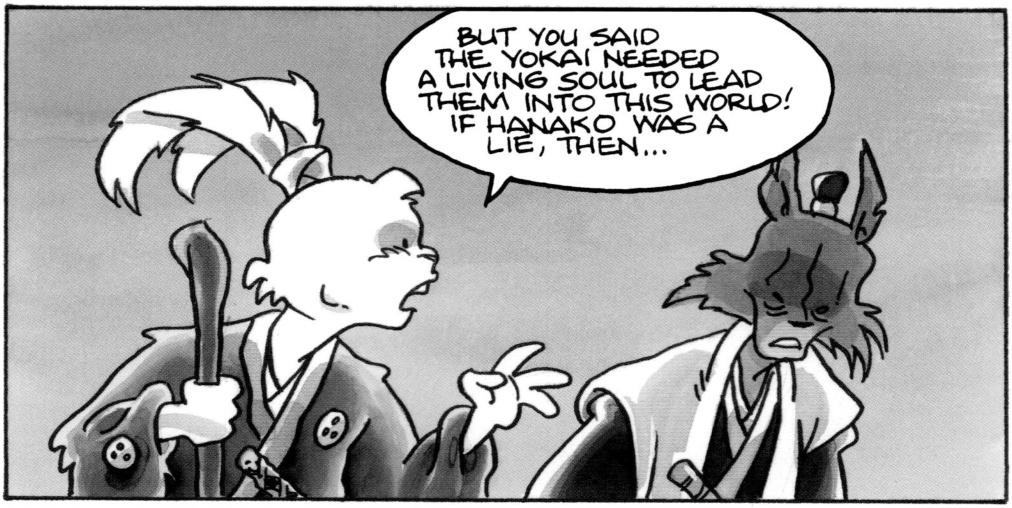
BUT YOU SAID THE YOKAI NEEDED A LIVING SOUL TO LEAD THEM INTO THIS WORLD! IF HANAKO WAS A LIE, THEN...

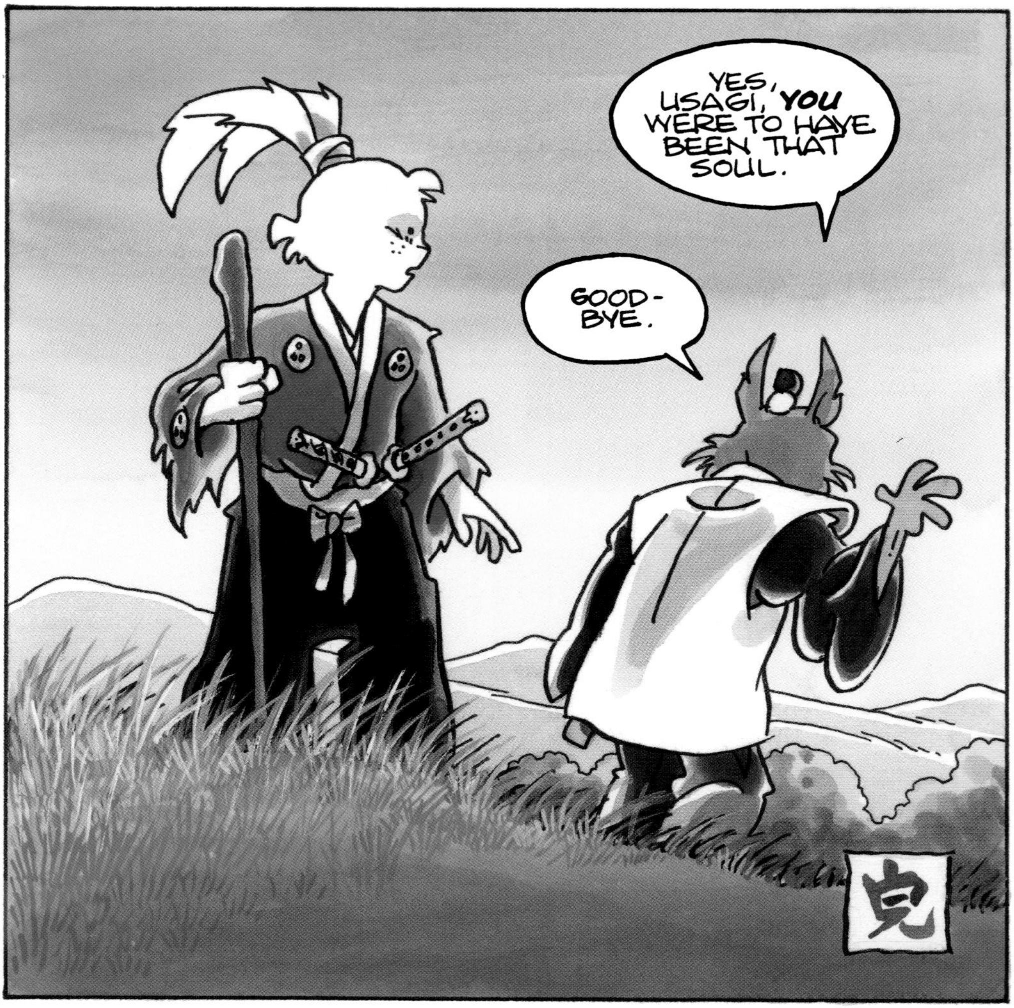
YES, USAGI, **YOU** WERE TO HAVE BEEN THAT SOUL.
GOOD-BYE.
完

THE *REAL* MAGIC BEHIND YOKAI
AN INTERVIEW WITH STAN SAKAI

坂井先生との対談

*U*SAGI YOJIMBO's *twenty-fifth anniversary demanded something truly special, and what could mark the occasion better than taking the opportunity to break new ground? Stan Sakai's covers for the* Usagi *book collections have showcased his incredible talent with watercolors, but Stan rarely has the chance to paint entire stories. In May, while he was finishing up* Yokai, *Stan talked to assistant editor Brendan Wright about the process of taking Miyamoto Usagi's world from black-and-white to fully painted color.*

Brendan Wright: *Was* Yokai *a story you'd been planning for the regular* Usagi *series, or did you come up with it once you knew you'd be creating this color graphic novel?*

Stan Sakai: I wrote it for the color graphic novel. I wanted the story to be special, because I had never done a painted story on this scale before. I needed a stand-alone story that those unfamiliar with Usagi could enjoy, but that would satisfy the longtime readers as well.

Japan has such a wonderful tradition of mythology and folklore, with not only the really horrific monsters, but also the goofy ones, such as the animated umbrella or the animated teapot. I wanted to do something with these creatures from folklore. There's the legend of "The Night Parade of One Hundred Demons," where every summer the demons get together and parade through towns, scaring people. On this particular night, however, they actually want to overrun and conquer Japan. But they need a living soul to guide them, so they kidnap a little girl, and her mother begs Usagi to rescue her. That's how the story of *Yokai* came about. I wanted Usagi to go through a wide range of emotions, so there's a lot of action, drama, and humor.

BW: *Some of the creatures in* Yokai *have shown up in* Usagi *before, but there are also plenty that you haven't used before. How did you select which ones you wanted to include?*

SS: I just picked the ones that looked cool. I went by their looks, powers, and background. I tried to keep a balance between the really monstrous ones and the really funny ones. There's one in particular called *sansho*, which is a leg from the shin down with a big eyeball and a shock

1. First, the story is pencilled on 5-ply Strathmore 500 series Bristol board.

2. Next, the art is inked with an art pen and Badger Black opaque ink. The borders are kept clean by masking them with tracing paper and rubber cement.

of hair on top. I love the design, and I think I've used it as a visual a couple of times, but I never really knew its background. I sent out a plea on the Internet, and it was picked up by a few of the comic book sites. Matt Alt, who had written a book called *Yokai Attack!*, e-mailed me and told me about it. It's actually a Chinese legend which was brought over to Japan.

BW: *Does good visual reference exist for all of the creatures in* Yokai*? Did you take many liberties or make changes from the folklore that they come from?*

SS: I took a lot of liberties, such as with the *sansho* I mentioned. Traditionally, it's just a leg with an eye, but I gave him a mouth because I needed him to be able to talk. Also, some of the creatures are just made up, because I love to draw monsters, and this time I was able to let my imagination go wild. The research for *Yokai* was more extensive than usual in that I had to go to a lot more sources for reference.

BW: Usagi *is primarily a black-and-white series. Are there differences you went for visually, knowing you'd have color?*

SS: I add a lot of texture [when working in] black-and-white. With the color book, I let the watercolors be the textures. I tend to work in planes—a foreground, middleground, and background—and with the watercolors I was able to play with that a lot more, such as bringing out the background, or trying to highlight the middleground. I think it comes from my love of animation, especially the old Disney stuff, where they would have the artwork on different levels.

BW: *What was your process for creating the painted pages?*

SS: It pretty much started the same as with black-and-white art. I wrote a script, or rather just a basic outline of a story, and then went to thumbnails. My thumbnails are usually my final script, and I worked out the pacing of this story at that stage. Then I went to pencils and inks. Now I'm just putting on the watercolors. This is the first time I'm doing so much painting, and that's something I really enjoy. As I'm progressing I think I'm getting better, getting looser with it.

BW: *Since your earlier painted stories, your style has changed quite a lot. The earliest story didn't have the ink outlines, and was more painterly. Since then you've developed the strong black outlines. Was that a conscious decision?*

SS: It was—mainly for speed, and also because I like the look of the black outlines. The first watercolor story I did, "Return to Adachi Plain," was completely done in watercolor, using just tone, and it took about a full month to do those eight pages. I only had two and a half months to do fifty-six pages for *Yokai*, so I had to work

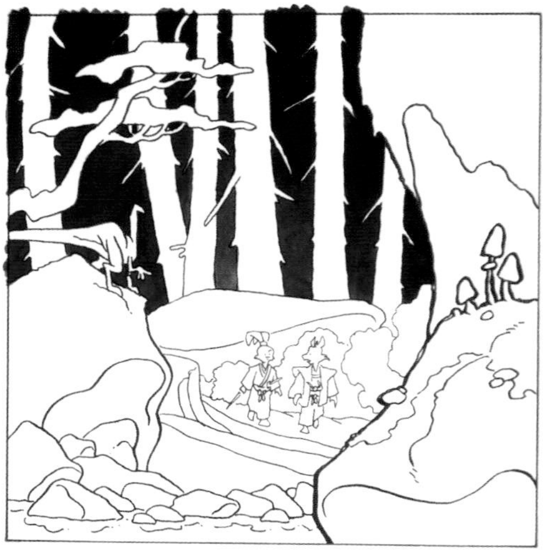

3. The painting begins with the dark blues in the background, and is done using Winsor & Newton watercolors and a #8 red sable brush.

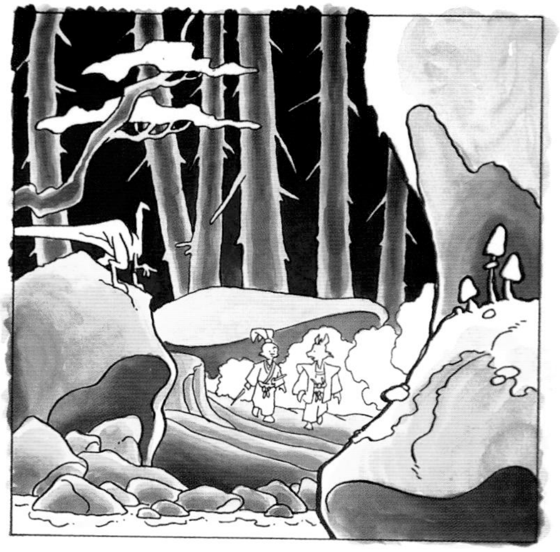

4. A range of earth tones is created using mixes of brown and yellow, with a touch of red for warmth.

quickly. The art does have a strong outline, but I try to let the color do as much of the work as possible.

BW: *You mentioned that you had less than three months. You're known for being really fast, but to write and draw and paint over fifty pages, that seems really, really fast. How long did each stage of that take?*

SS: The writing, pencilling, and inking took about three weeks or so, and the rest of the time has been spent painting. I'm getting faster with the painting as I'm going along. It also helps that I'm working at a slightly smaller size, and there are fewer panels per page. The regular *Usagi* stories average five or six panels per page. With *Yokai* I'm working with three and four panels.

BW: *What was your emphasis in art school? Did you study painting? Did you draw comics at all?*

SS: No, no comics at all. My major at the University of Hawaii was drawing and painting, and the emphasis at that time was on Abstract Expressionism, mainly with acrylics and oils. I love working with oils, but of course they take such a long time. I would not have been able to do a fifty-six-page story in oil paints.

I never studied watercolors, and I wish I'd had that opportunity. At the Art Center it was mainly advertising and illustration, and the emphasis there was working with markers. I've never liked markers. I'm really happy working with watercolors. It's so much freer and much more expressive.

BW: *This type of art, using watercolors to color well-defined linework, is not very common in American comics. What were some sources of inspiration for your own process?*

SS: It's a lot more common in European graphic novels, and that's something I really got into after college, when I first discovered *Asterix*. Later, *Heavy Metal* [published] Moebius's work, and that just floored me. I've been fortunate to travel to Europe quite often, so whenever I'm there I pick up some graphic albums, especially the French ones, such as *Blacksad*—it's great. There's also Hermann's stuff, especially his Medieval series—it's done pretty much the same way, with an ink outline and watercolor paintings. As I said, this approach is pretty common in Europe, and that was my inspiration for the way I painted *Yokai*.

BW: Yokai *is one of the projects commemorating your twenty-fifth anniversary of writing and drawing* Usagi. *What keeps you inspired to return to this world, and to keep expanding it with new characters and new settings?*

SS: I really enjoy working with *Usagi*. I enjoy working with the characters, I enjoy writing the stories, and I enjoy the drawing. I get to work at home, watch TV while

5. The vegetation and the tokage lizard are colored using a mixture of green and a small amount of turquoise. A touch of orange is added for the grayer tones.

6. Next, Usagi, the water, and the treetops are painted turquoise.

I'm working—it's great. There's no commute time at all! I take a break whenever I want to. But every so often, I'll get a call from Diana [Schutz, *Usagi*'s editor] saying, "Hey, you're late." Then I really have to play catch-up.

BW: *Over the twenty-five years, how has making* Usagi *changed, either in the process or working with the characters?*

SS: I've gotten more comfortable with the character, as well as the process of doing comic books. When I first started out, I remember doing an eight-page Usagi story, and it took me a month to do, and I thought, "Wow, this is great. I really whipped that out." But now I've got to finish twenty-four pages every five weeks, so I've gotten faster. Also, working with Sergio Aragonés sped me up a lot, mostly through years of ridicule: "You work so slowly, you've got to speed it up. What? You have to pencil?"

Usagi has changed, and a lot of it is unconscious on my part. When he started out, his physical proportions were much different. Right now he seems taller, which appeals to me a lot more, because somehow it goes with the more dramatic stories that I've been telling. His personality has changed, too, in very subtle ways, but he has matured over the years, just as I think I've matured as a storyteller.

BW: *How about the fans? What's your interaction with the fan community like?*

SS: Oh, the fans are wonderful. They set up a wonderful website at usagiyojimbo.com. *Usagi* fans are very generous, not only those in the U.S., but internationally as well. I went to France once, and one of the French fans took a week off from work to escort me to sights that I wanted to see, as well as to a convention. The fans are just great.

BW: Usagi *is a series that a lot of people have followed for the entire twenty-five years. Is it humbling that* Usagi *has been a part of so many people's lives for so long?*

SS: Oh, yeah. Yeah, I've gotten letters saying that *Usagi*'s used in schools, or from people who discovered *Usagi* at the library and now are hooked on it. *Grasscutter* was used as a textbook in Japanese History classes at the University of Portland in Oregon. That's pretty neat. And there've been theses written about *Usagi*, so it's been very humbling.

BW: *Is there anything about the series or about* Yokai *that you want to add?*

SS: Just that I'm looking forward to the next twenty-five years! I have stories written down the line, and each story I write is a springboard for two more. I'm having fun with it.

7. Details like the mushrooms and Usagi's hakama pants come next. Sasuke and the foreground rocks are painted a yellow ochre, and a light turquoise wash pushes the other rocks into the background.

8. White cel vinyl is added to highlights and used to make corrections. Finally, the border mask is peeled off.

Stan celebrates twenty-five years of Usagi at the Pacific Asia Museum in Pasadena. *Photo by Sharon Sakai*

坂井 **STAN SAKAI** was born in Kyoto, Japan, grew up in Hawaii, and now lives in California with his wife, Sharon, and two children, Hannah and Matthew. He received a Fine Arts degree from the University of Hawaii and furthered his studies at Art Center College of Design in Pasadena, California.

His creation, Usagi Yojimbo, first appeared in comics in 1984. Since then, Usagi has been on television as a guest of the Teenage Mutant Ninja Turtles and has been made into toys, seen on clothing, and featured in a series of graphic novel collections.

In 1991, Stan created *Space Usagi*, a series dealing with samurai in a futuristic setting, featuring the adventures of a descendant of the original Usagi.

Stan is also an award-winning letterer for his work on Sergio Aragonés' *Groo*, the "Spider-Man" Sunday newspaper strips, and *Usagi Yojimbo*.

Stan is a recipient of a Parents' Choice Award, an Inkpot Award, an American Library Association Award, a Harvey Award, four Spanish Haxtur Awards, and several Eisner Awards. In 2003 he received the prestigious National Cartoonists Society Award in the Comic Book Division.

Editor
DIANA SCHUTZ

Assistant Editor
BRENDAN WRIGHT

Digital Production
RYAN HILL

Designer
CARY GRAZZINI

Publisher
MIKE RICHARDSON

兎用心棒:妖怪

USAGI YOJIMBO™ : YOKAI

Library of Congress Cataloging-in-Publication Data on file.

Visit the Usagi Yojimbo Dojo website
usagiyojimbo.com

Published by Dark Horse Books
A division of Dark Horse Comics, Inc.
10956 SE Main Street
Milwaukie, Oregon 97222
darkhorse.com

First edition: November 2009
ISBN 978-1-59582-362-5

1 3 5 7 9 10 8 6 4 2
PRINTED IN CHINA

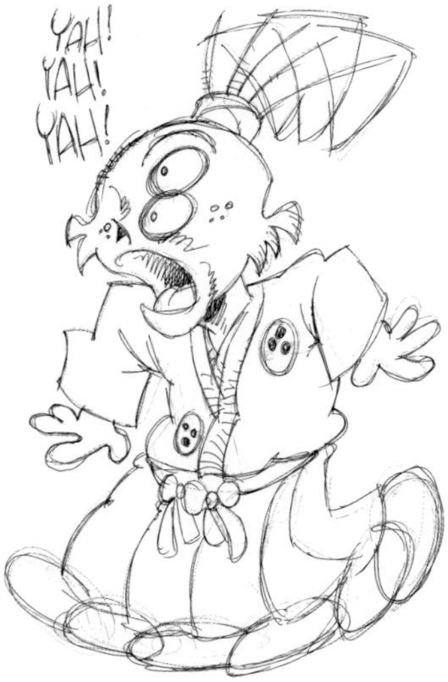
YAH! YAH! YAH!

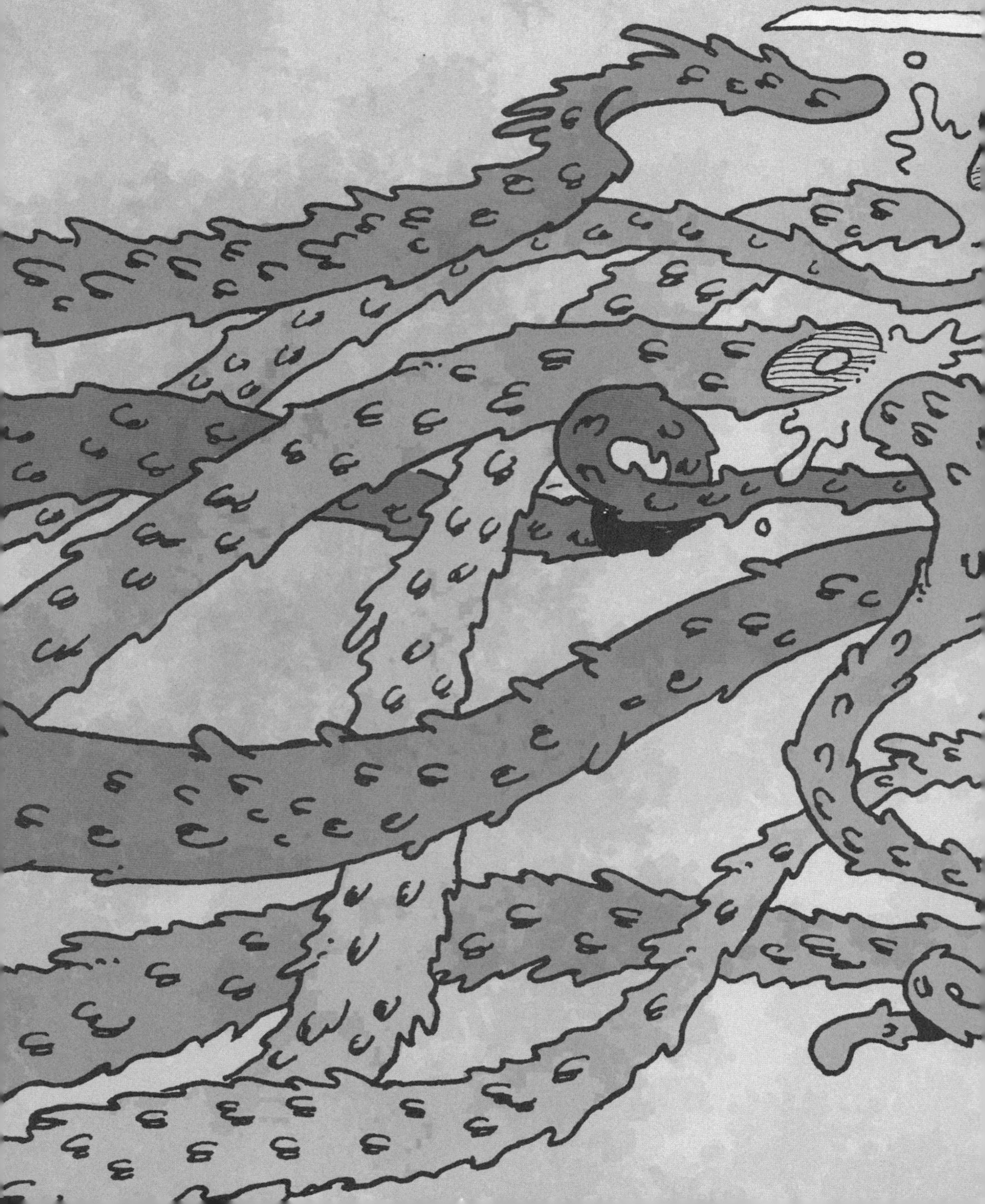